LUDERE LATINE I

BY PAUL O'BRIEN

Coordinated with
Latina Christiana I

Additional Discounted Copies of *Ludere Latine*

If you purchased this book NEW:
You may order additional bound *Ludere Latine* books online for less than the cost of copying. To order additional discounted books, go to
www.MemoriaPress.com/copy

Ludere Latine I: Latin Games & Puzzles
by Paul O'Brien

© 2006 Memoria Press
ISBN #: 978-1-930953-97-0

Memoria Press
www.memoriapress.com

INTRODUCTION

The Latin word games in this book are both fun and instructive. They are coordinated with the vocabulary and grammar in the lessons of Latina Christiana I, an elementary Latin course available in book and video from Memoria Press. Ludere Latine can be a supplemental learning aid for students using the Latina Christiana course. It may also be used independently by any beginning student of Latin.

There are several types of games.

Word Search. The player finds each of the clue words in a matrix of letters. The Latin words may be hidden in the matrix in any orientation -- vertical, horizontal, diagonal, forwards or backwards. This game promotes the learning of Latin vocabulary.

Derivatives Crossword. The clue is a Latin word. The player finds an English derivative of this word that fits in the crossword. As each Latin clue word may have several English derivatives, the game promotes acquisition of English vocabulary and the understanding of roots. Some of the derivatives can be found in the Latina Christiana I lesson. Additional derivatives are given in a hint box with the game.

Grammar Crossword. The clue words are in English. The player translates the word into Latin in its correct grammatical form to complete the crossword.

Parse Strings. The player matches Latin words with grammatical parsings (case, number, tense, and so on).

Hangman. The paper version needs two people. The player offers a letter. The other person, checking the answer key, determines if the letter fits any of the blanks. If so, the player enters the letter in the appropriate blank(s). If not, the player hangs a part of the man on the gallows (head, neck, torso, arms, legs). The player tries to guess the correct Latin phrase before the hanging man is complete.

At the end of the book are rules for five group games that can be played by students, either in the classroom or at home.

Contents

LESSON 1

WORD SEARCH

Find the 5 vocabulary words of Lesson 1 in the matrix.

```
F F P Q K L B R
T K J M N A L G
X O X N O B X G
N M P T H O R V
J A R C D R R K
K O M W W O V O
P W M V T X N X
H G L A U D O G
```

amo
porto
laudo
oro
laboro

1

Derivatives Crossword

Complete the crossword using derivatives of the clue words.

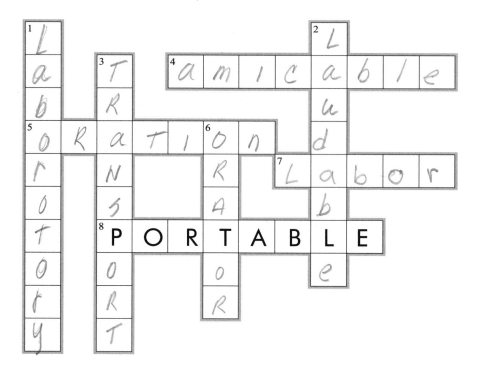

Across
4. amo
5. oro
7. laboro
8. porto

Down
1. laboro
2. laudo
3. porto
6. oro

Here are some additional derivatives of Latin words in this lesson. Some of them may fit in the crossword. Can you guess which Latin words they come from? Be sure to look up the definitions of supplementary derivatives in the Vocabulary section, beginning on page 151.

labor   amicable
oratorical   oration
amiable

LESSON 2

WORD SEARCH

Find the 10 vocabulary words of Lesson 2 in the matrix.

```
H T R V N A W L M H
Y V G T I R O E B O
Y V K L P T M Z Z R
G O A Y C O A A L A
N T G E R M N M T P
I L P I T F W O R C
V S A Q V D C R M A
V N G V H A T M Q Q
G L O R I A N H Z U
K A I R O T C I V A
```

Roma   memoria
Italia   victoria
gloria   navigo
vita   paro
aqua   specto

1 you talking
2. Talking to about
3. talking about

PARSE STRINGS

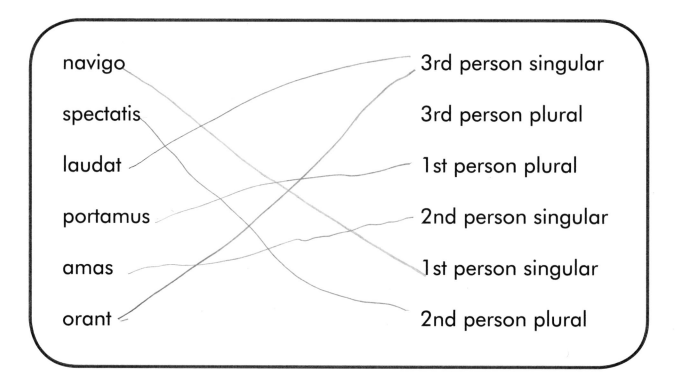

navigo   3rd person singular

spectatis   3rd person plural

laudat   1st person plural

portamus   2nd person singular

amas   1st person singular

orant   2nd person plural

For the Parse Strings game, you will need to know the names of the grammatical features of verbs, such as person and number. Here is the table for the present tense, using the verb <u>amo</u>.

	singular	plural	
	I	*we*	
1st person:	amo *o*	amamus	*mus*
	you	*you*	
2nd person:	amas *s*	amatis	*tis*
	he she it	*they*	
3rd person:	amat *t*	amant	*nt*

You can see that <u>amamus</u> is 1st person plural, and <u>amat</u> is 3rd person singular. Try to figure out the rest of the answers. You may need to refer back to this table for future Parse Strings.

Derivatives Crossword

Complete the crossword using derivatives of the clue words.

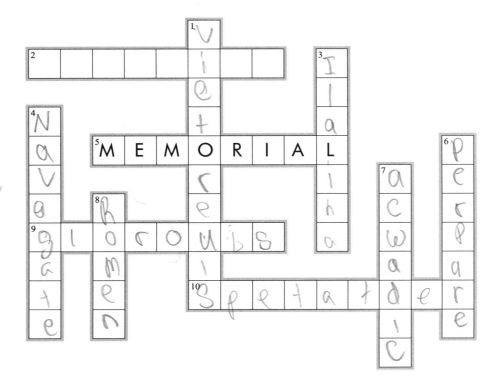

Across
2.   vita
5.   memoria
9.   gloria
10.   specto

Down
1.   victoria
3.   Italia
4.   navigo
6.   paro
7.   aqua
8.   Roma

Here are some additional derivatives of Latin words in this lesson. Some of them may fit in the crossword. Can you guess which Latin words they come from?

revitalize   Roman   preparatory

Italian   vitality   prepare

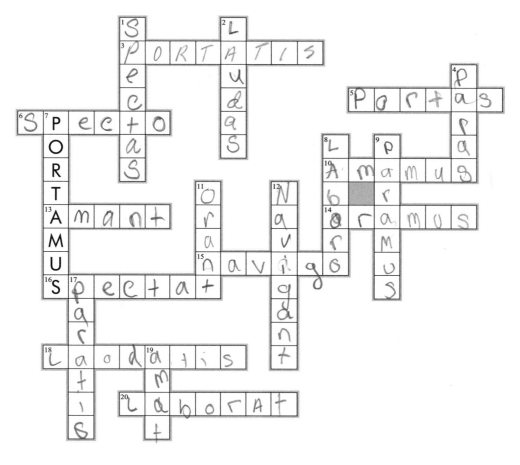

Grammar Crossword

Enter the correct grammatical form.

Across

3. you (pl.) carry
5. you carry
6. I look at
10. we love
13. they love
14. we pray
15. I sail
16. she looks at
18. you (pl.) praise
20. she works

Down

1. you look at
2. you praise
4. you prepare
7. we carry
8. I work
9. we prepare
11. they pray
12. they sail
17. you (pl.) prepare
19. he loves

LESSON 3

WORD SEARCH

Find the 10 vocabulary words of Lesson 3 in the matrix.

T Q W C N X A L F M
O C F T L U K A P J
P M Z O G X N R O K
X K A N R N R R H N
R F I L A T E E E P
Q L Q U C P U T R T
M B T X U L O N B C
M A L S L K C Z A V
N F T P C C O V I A
A I L L A G V V N T

terra   nauta
lingua   Gallia
via   clamo
fortuna   voco
herba   supero

3

PARSE STRINGS

vocant	1st person singular
laboramus	3rd person singular
superatis	1st person plural
porto	2nd person singular
clamat	3rd person plural
spectas	2nd person plural

Derivatives Crossword

Complete the crossword using derivatives of the clue words.

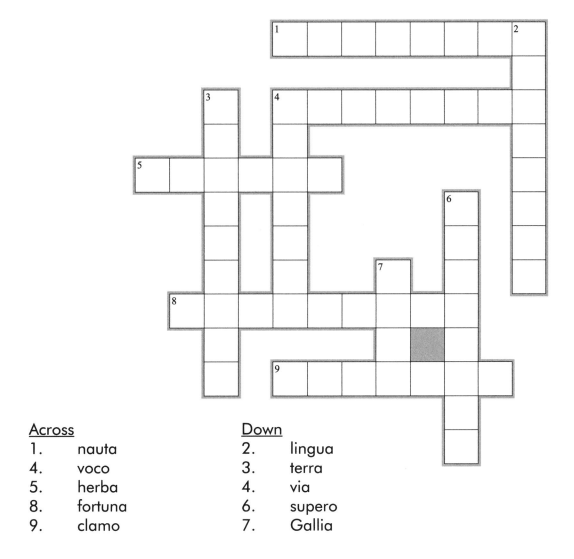

Across
1. nauta
4. voco
5. herba
8. fortuna
9. clamo

Down
2. lingua
3. terra
4. via
6. supero
7. Gallia

Here are some additional derivatives of Latin words in this lesson. Some of them may fit in the crossword. Can you guess which Latin words they come from?

herbal	claim	Gaul
exclaim	herbicide	disclaim

3

Grammar Crossword

Across

3. we prepare
5. I shout
7. you work
9. he prepares
10. we love
12. he calls
15. you (pl.) praise
16. you (pl.) shout
18. we call
20. I overcome

Down

1. she sails
2. they work
4. you (pl.) sail
6. you call
8. they overcome
11. you (pl.) carry
13. they shout
14. you look at
17. you love
19. I pray

LESSON 4

WORD SEARCH

Find the number words of Lesson 4 in the matrix.

```
C  C  R  O  U  T  T  A  U  Q
W  T  T  C  M  S  O  R  R  K
N  Q  M  F  E  I  B  T  Y  J
S  L  U  P  S  M  L  O  C  T
E  P  T  I  U  K  U  L  M  O
X  E  K  T  N  D  F  C  E  X
M  X  N  G  U  Q  N  R  V  L
T  E  M  M  R  K  U  L  O  G
C  R  T  R  E  S  N  E  N  D
M  K  N  F  D  E  C  E  M  L
```

unus	sex
duo	septem
tres	octo
quattuor	novem
quinque	decem

centum
mille

4

PARSE STRINGS

es	1st person singular
sumus	3rd person singular
est	1st person plural
sunt	2nd person singular
sum	3rd person plural
estis	2nd person plural

Derivatives Crossword

Complete the crossword using derivatives of the clue words.

Across
3. septem
5. octo
6. duo
7. tres
8. quinque
10. novem
11. quattuor
12. unus

Down
1. centum
2. decem
4. mille
9. sex

Here are some additional derivatives of Latin words in this lesson. Some of them may fit in the crossword. Can you guess which Latin words they come from?

quintet   sextet   octet

4

Grammar Crossword

Across

1. I shout
4. I love
5. I prepare
7. you (pl.) shout
11. they are
12. you work
15. it is
16. you are
17. I am
18. she shouts
19. we are
20. you call

Down

2. you (pl.) pray
3. they call
6. they praise
8. you (pl.) look at
9. we call
10. it carries
11. we conquer
13. she overcomes
14. we sail
16. you (pl.) are

LESSON 5

WORD SEARCH

Find the 10 words of Lesson 5 in the matrix.

```
R  B  R  E  G  I  N  A  M  O
L  O  V  H  H  C  A  V  F  R
P  R  R  K  Y  I  A  R  Z  E
U  N  Y  O  L  V  N  M  B  B
E  L  M  I  D  O  I  L  L  I
L  G  F  E  L  A  M  V  Z  L
L  T  D  U  N  X  E  H  W  T
A  B  B  M  Z  S  F  K  O  G
C  M  X  R  G  T  A  G  F  T
A  I  R  T  A  P  A  J  M  Z
```

femina   toga
filia   patria
regina   adoro
mensa   libero
puella   ambulo

5

Derivatives Crossword

Complete the crossword using derivatives of the clue words.

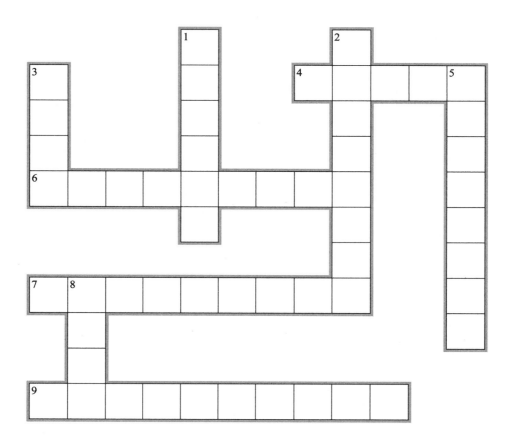

Across
4.   regina
6.   adoro
7.   ambulo
9.   patria

Down
1.   filia
2.   femina
3.   toga
5.   libero
8.   mensa

Here are some additional derivatives of Latin words in this lesson. Some of them may fit in the crossword. Can you guess which Latin words they come from?

regalia	toga	patriotism
adore	regal	ambulatory

Grammar Crossword

Across

1. girl
3. daughter
4. woman
9. she praises
10. we are
11. they work
12. we adore
14. he is
15. we pray
17. you (pl.) look at
18. they adore
19. you adore
21. I overcome
23. it frees
25. I free
26. she walks
27. you prepare

Down

1. you carry
2. he sails
5. table
6. you (pl.) call
7. country
8. we walk
11. you (pl.) free
13. they are
16. they shout
18. I love
20. you walk
22. queen
24. toga

Latin Sayings Hangman

_ _ _ _ R _ _ _ _ N _ _

_ _ O _ O _ _ _ _ _ _ _ _ _

_ _ T _ _ _ T _ _ _ _ _ _ _ _ _

_ _ _ _ _ _ _ _ T _ T _ _ _ _

_ _ _ _ T _ B _ _ _ _ _

LESSON 6

WORD SEARCH

Find the 10 words of Lesson 6 in the matrix.

```
A  V  L  I  S  R  G  R  T  R
L  P  O  K  Q  Z  B  H  M  O
Z  R  X  N  M  L  I  X  P  C
J  H  D  N  G  S  U  U  R  I
F  U  G  A  P  U  C  N  J  D
M  P  U  A  K  C  P  A  A  U
L  L  N  K  O  M  I  M  P  J
H  I  D  G  J  R  L  N  L  P
A  J  A  V  A  Y  H  C  U  K
T  G  W  M  B  K  Q  C  C  W
```

culpa	Hispania
Maria	silva
fuga	pugno
luna	judico
unda	occupo

6

PARSE STRINGS

lunae	accusative singular
Hispaniam	genitive plural
culpa	genitive singular
silvarum	accusative plural
culpis	dative plural
undas	nominative singular

For the Parse Strings game, you will need to know the names of the grammatical features of nouns, such as case and number. Here is the table for the first declension, using the noun <u>luna</u>.

	<u>singular</u>	<u>plural</u>
nominative case:	luna	lunae
genitive case:	lunae	lunarum
dative case:	lunae	lunis
accusative case:	lunam	lunas
ablative case:	luna	lunis

Here you can see that <u>lunam</u> is the accusative singular, and <u>lunis</u> is either the dative plural or the ablative plural.

Derivatives Crossword

Complete the crossword using derivatives of the clue words.

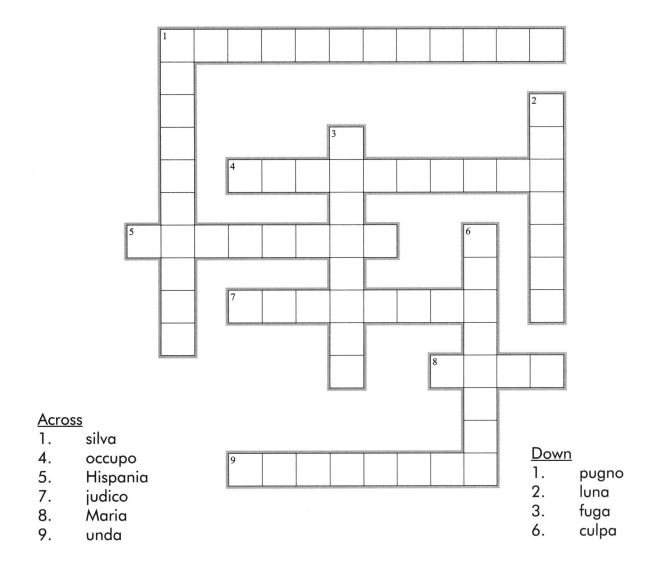

Across
1.   silva
4.   occupo
5.   Hispania
7.   judico
8.   Maria
9.   unda

Down
1.   pugno
2.   luna
3.   fuga
6.   culpa

Here are some additional derivatives of Latin words in this lesson. Some of them may fit in the crossword. Can you guess which Latin words they come from?

Mary   judge   judicial

Grammar Crossword

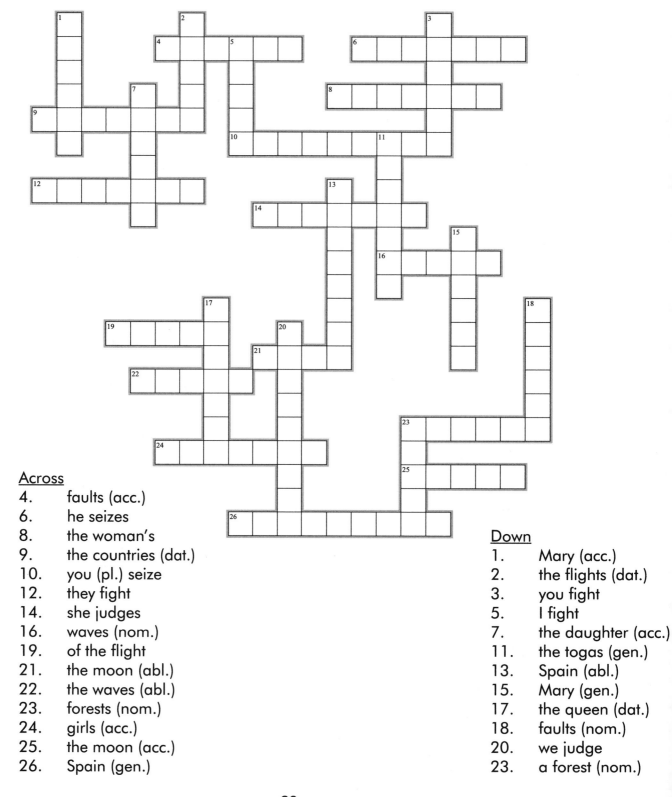

Across
4. faults (acc.)
6. he seizes
8. the woman's
9. the countries (dat.)
10. you (pl.) seize
12. they fight
14. she judges
16. waves (nom.)
19. of the flight
21. the moon (abl.)
22. the waves (abl.)
23. forests (nom.)
24. girls (acc.)
25. the moon (acc.)
26. Spain (gen.)

Down
1. Mary (acc.)
2. the flights (dat.)
3. you fight
5. I fight
7. the daughter (acc.)
11. the togas (gen.)
13. Spain (abl.)
15. Mary (gen.)
17. the queen (dat.)
18. faults (nom.)
20. we judge
23. a forest (nom.)

LESSON 7

WORD SEARCH

Find the 10 words of Lesson 7 in the matrix.

```
L A S J H V R W J W
L M J E K H M R A M
M I E T R B Y A L R
K C T S N V S B L Y
K U N C U R U K E C
L S A L U N A S T C
I R A H W N I S S D
Y V R D N K O M C V
X N P U D P C M O L
M V S U I L I F R D
```

stella   annus
ursa   filius
ira   dominus
servus   ante
amicus   post

PARSE STRINGS

lunam	accusative plural
puellarum	dative plural
toga	genitive plural
silvas	ablative singular
stellae	accusative singular
ursis	nominative plural

Derivatives Crossword

Complete the crossword using derivatives of the clue words.

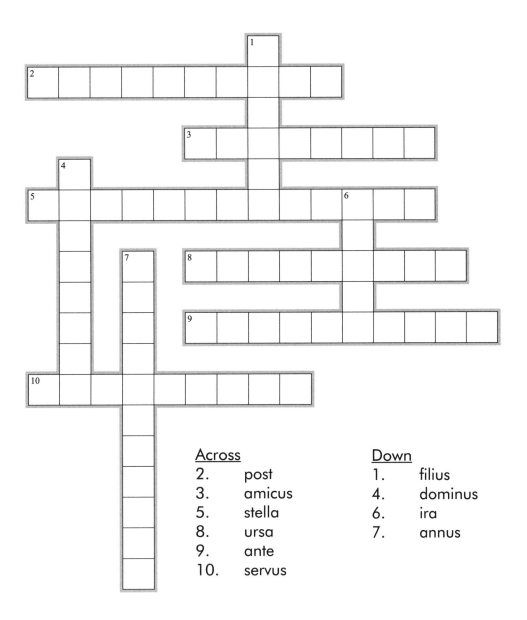

Across
2.   post
3.   amicus
5.   stella
8.   ursa
9.   ante
10. servus

Down
1.   filius
4.   dominus
6.   ira
7.   annus

Here are some additional derivatives of Latin words in this lesson. Some of them may fit in the crossword. Can you guess which Latin words they come from?

postscript	domination	servitude
anticipate	antebellum	domain

7

Grammar Crossword

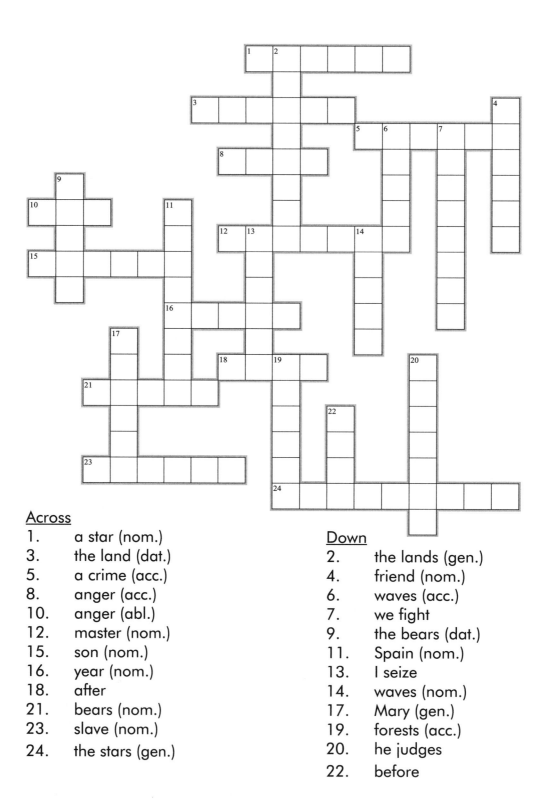

Across

1. a star (nom.)
3. the land (dat.)
5. a crime (acc.)
8. anger (acc.)
10. anger (abl.)
12. master (nom.)
15. son (nom.)
16. year (nom.)
18. after
21. bears (nom.)
23. slave (nom.)
24. the stars (gen.)

Down

2. the lands (gen.)
4. friend (nom.)
6. waves (acc.)
7. we fight
9. the bears (dat.)
11. Spain (nom.)
13. I seize
14. waves (nom.)
17. Mary (gen.)
19. forests (acc.)
20. he judges
22. before

LESSON 8

WORD SEARCH

Find the 10 words of Lesson 8 in the matrix.

```
G  J  C  G  A  J  R  S  D  Z
S  F  N  Q  Y  R  U  R  I  R
U  N  B  F  E  T  O  Q  S  E
E  L  A  P  S  N  M  H  C  P
D  M  E  I  V  C  D  J  I  M
A  A  R  G  Y  N  Y  R  P  E
S  H  Z  N  A  J  E  S  U  S
C  Q  T  G  N  T  N  R  L  K
K  W  C  M  F  T  U  Z  U  H
A  I  T  A  R  G  Q  S  S  T
```

Deus	fama
Christus	gratia
Jesus	hora
legatus	semper
discipulus	saepe

8

PARSE STRINGS

legatos	ablative singular
Deum	accusative plural
horis	genitive singular
discipuli	accusative singular
Christus	dative plural
Deo	nominative singular

8

Derivatives Crossword

Complete the crossword using derivatives of the clue words.

Across
3. gratia
6. discipulus
8. Deus
10. fama
11. Christus
12. hora
13. discipulus

Down
1. fama
2. legatus
4. Deus
5. legatus
7. Christus
9. gratia

Here are some additional derivatives of Latin words in this lesson. Some of them may fit in the crossword. Can you guess which Latin words they come from?

hour	Christian	legation
Christmas	deify	fame
infamy	grace	grateful

Grammar Crossword

<u>Across</u>
1. the students (gen.)
4. a slave (dat.)
5. hours (nom.)
7. hours (abl.)
8. Jesus (nom.)
10. hours (acc.)
13. God (acc.)
16. the envoys (abl.)
19. rumors (abl.)
22. grace (acc.)
23. students (nom.)

<u>Down</u>
1. the gods (gen.)
2. rumors (nom.)
3. Christ (nom.)
4. always
6. grace (gen.)
9. often
11. the slaves (acc.)
12. fame (abl.)
13. the student (acc.)
14. the envoys (gen.)
15. a lieutenant (acc.)

17. Christ (gen.)
18. grace (nom.)
20. the slave (gen.)
21. God (gen.)

LESSON 9

WORD SEARCH

Find the 10 words of Lesson 9 in the matrix.

```
R  P  L  U  D  U  S  G  S  A
Q  L  O  M  F  T  P  M  U  N
G  G  N  P  Z  Y  S  M  I  I
A  G  V  K  U  U  C  P  D  M
A  L  V  N  R  L  E  N  A  U
N  L  I  U  F  C  U  R  L  S
O  N  M  U  U  C  O  S  G  F
R  T  D  N  Q  M  T  V  Q  H
O  R  I  K  J  A  N  X  P  M
C  A  A  I  S  E  L  C  C  E
```

gladius	pecunia
murus	ecclesia
ludus	aquila
populus	corona
animus	mora

PARSE STRINGS

populo	2nd person singular
moras	accusative singular
pugnat	1st person singular
ludorum	3rd person singular
judicamus	ablative plural
occupant	2nd person plural
animi	genitive plural
gladiis	dative singular
vocas	3rd person plural
clamo	nominative singular
murum	genitive singular
judicatis	accusative plural
pecunia	1st person plural

Derivatives Crossword

Complete the crossword using derivatives of the clue words.

Across
2. aquila
3. gladius
7. populus
8. ecclesia
9. animus
10. mora

Down
1. ludus
4. corona
5. murus
6. pecunia

Here are some additional derivatives of Latin words in this lesson. Some of them may fit in the crossword. Can you guess which Latin words they come from?

populous   animation   prelude

9

Grammar Crossword

Across

2. money (gen.)
4. an eagle (dat.)
7. delays (acc.)
9. a game (acc.)
10. the peoples (gen.)
14. the games (acc.)
16. churches (nom.)
17. crowns (nom.)
19. crown (acc.)
21. spirits (abl.)
22. wall (nom.)
23. the walls (abl.)
24. swords (acc.)
26. eagles (dat.)
27. money (acc.)
28. the game (gen.)
29. the crowns (gen.)

Down

1. the walls (gen.)
3. the spirit (acc.)
5. eagles (acc.)
6. the people (acc.)
8. the people (gen.)
11. delays (nom.)
12. the churches (gen.)
13. money (abl.)
15. swords (nom.)
18. church (acc.)
20. spirit (nom.)
22. delay (nom.)
25. a sword (abl.)

LESSON 10

WORD SEARCH

Find the 10 words of Lesson 10 in the matrix.

```
S  U  B  I  C  L  F  M  S  M
B  L  M  B  Q  S  M  U  R  C
W  A  D  S  U  B  I  V  C  A
S  L  R  C  U  C  M  A  S  M
U  C  O  B  O  U  P  F  U  P
D  L  Y  S  A  I  Q  K  T  U
N  K  Y  D  L  R  C  E  N  S
U  M  K  L  G  B  U  N  E  F
M  N  U  N  T  I  U  S  V  G
M  S  R  N  Q  T  L  Q  L  W
```

mundus	capillus
socius	cibus
nuntius	equus
barbarus	ventus
campus	locus

PARSE STRINGS

nuntii   ablative singular

ventorum   accusative plural

socius   genitive singular

mundo   accusative singular

equis   genitive plural

campum   nominative singular

capillos   dative plural

Derivatives Crossword

Complete the crossword using derivatives of the clue words.

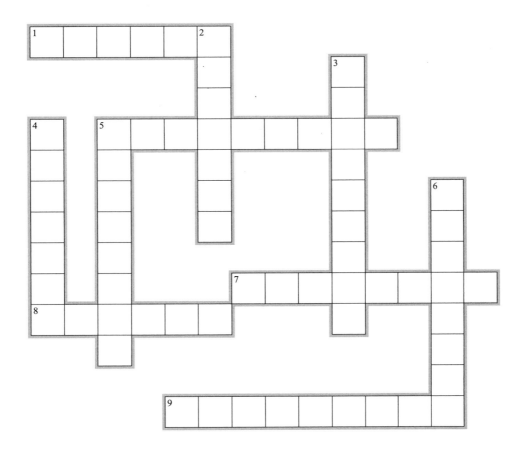

Across		Down	
1.	campus	2.	socius
5.	capillus	3.	barbarus
7.	locus	4.	mundus
8.	equus	5.	cibus
9.	ventus	6.	nuntius

Here are some additional derivatives of Latin words in this lesson. Some of them may fit in the crossword. Can you guess which Latin words they come from?

campus   barbarian   locality

10

Grammar Crossword

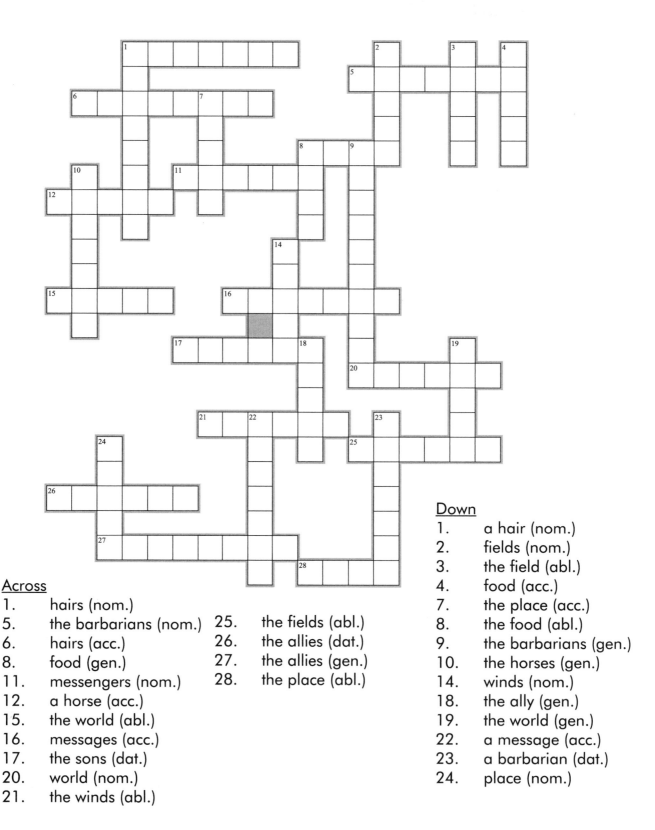

Across

1. hairs (nom.)
5. the barbarians (nom.)
6. hairs (acc.)
8. food (gen.)
11. messengers (nom.)
12. a horse (acc.)
15. the world (abl.)
16. messages (acc.)
17. the sons (dat.)
20. world (nom.)
21. the winds (abl.)
25. the fields (abl.)
26. the allies (dat.)
27. the allies (gen.)
28. the place (abl.)

Down

1. a hair (nom.)
2. fields (nom.)
3. the field (abl.)
4. food (acc.)
7. the place (acc.)
8. the food (abl.)
9. the barbarians (gen.)
10. the horses (gen.)
14. winds (nom.)
18. the ally (gen.)
19. the world (gen.)
22. a message (acc.)
23. a barbarian (dat.)
24. place (nom.)

Latin Sayings Hangman

_ _ _ O _ O _ _ _ _

_ _ _ _ _ _ _ _ _ P _ P _ _ _ _ _
_ _ _ _ _ _

_ _ _ P _ _ _ _ N _ _ _

_ E _ _ _ _ P _

S _ _ _ _ _ _ _ _ _ _ _ S

LESSON 11

WORD SEARCH

Find the 10 words of Lesson 11 in the matrix.

```
N  K  R  D  M  Z  K  W  P  R  M  M
V  R  J  U  R  J  T  K  R  C  M  P
K  N  N  P  J  L  Y  N  K  N  U  K
N  O  L  O  P  P  I  D  U  M  I  F
D  T  L  M  U  T  N  E  M  U  R  F
N  M  E  N  Y  K  R  W  M  J  E  V
D  H  U  L  X  T  R  R  U  K  P  E
V  M  Q  N  U  E  D  W  L  X  M  R
N  R  N  H  G  M  Z  W  L  F  I  B
L  Z  L  N  N  I  Y  G  E  K  R  U
L  D  U  D  L  V  S  T  B  P  B  M
C  M  P  K  M  U  I  L  E  O  R  P
```

bellum	regnum
donum	frumentum
oppidum	signum
telum	imperium
verbum	proelium

11

PARSE STRINGS

verbis	accusative singular
imperii	nominative plural
regna	genitive plural
oppido	ablative plural
signum	genitive singular
bellorum	ablative singular

Derivatives Crossword

Complete the crossword using derivatives of the clue words.

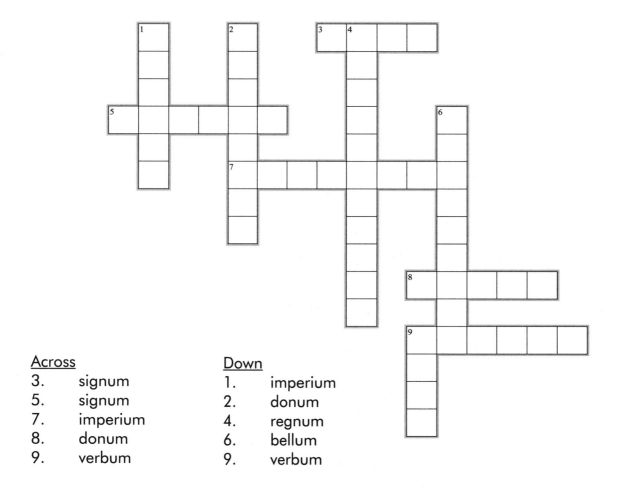

Across
3. signum
5. signum
7. imperium
8. donum
9. verbum

Down
1. imperium
2. donum
4. regnum
6. bellum
9. verbum

Here are some additional derivatives of Latin words in this lesson. Some of them may fit in the crossword. Can you guess which Latin words they come from?

rebellion   interregnum   sign

Grammar Crossword

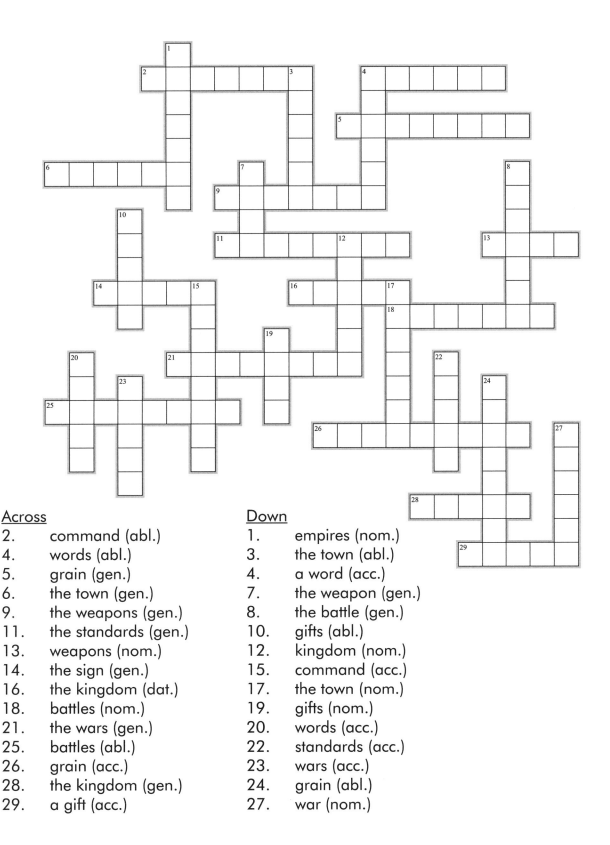

Across
2. command (abl.)
4. words (abl.)
5. grain (gen.)
6. the town (gen.)
9. the weapons (gen.)
11. the standards (gen.)
13. weapons (nom.)
14. the sign (gen.)
16. the kingdom (dat.)
18. battles (nom.)
21. the wars (gen.)
25. battles (abl.)
26. grain (acc.)
28. the kingdom (gen.)
29. a gift (acc.)

Down
1. empires (nom.)
3. the town (abl.)
4. a word (acc.)
7. the weapon (gen.)
8. the battle (gen.)
10. gifts (abl.)
12. kingdom (nom.)
15. command (acc.)
17. the town (nom.)
19. gifts (nom.)
20. words (acc.)
22. standards (acc.)
23. wars (acc.)
24. grain (abl.)
27. war (nom.)

LESSON 12

WORD SEARCH

Find the 10 words of Lesson 12 in the matrix.

```
T  Z  M  U  I  I  M  E  A  R  P  M  F
N  D  E  B  I  T  U  M  V  U  U  Y  M
P  Q  H  T  N  P  H  C  I  Q  L  U
E  N  Y  D  N  W  Y  L  L  T  R  G
C  C  K  B  M  C  I  T  V  X  Y  R
C  W  M  C  G  X  A  A  M  T  K  E
A  W  U  M  U  M  L  E  M  R  T  T
T  X  I  A  J  L  U  M  L  F  T  K
U  C  D  K  U  L  U  N  M  U  J  K
M  X  U  M  Y  R  H  B  I  L  M  M
B  P  A  T  O  Z  L  Q  T  V  M  T
T  M  G  F  Q  X  R  L  J  N  N  M
```

gaudium	vallum
auxilium	praemium
debitum	vinum
caelum	tergum
peccatum	forum

50

PARSE STRINGS

gaudium	genitive plural neuter
mundis	accusative singular neuter
vino	accusative plural masculine
ventum	nominative plural neuter
vallorum	dative singular masculine
barbarorum	nominative plural masculine
equo	genitive singular neuter
campi	ablative singular neuter
fora	ablative plural neuter
auxilii	accusative singular masculine
dominos	nominative singular masculine
verbis	ablative plural masculine
filius	genitive plural masculine

12

Derivatives Crossword

Complete the crossword using derivatives of the clue words.

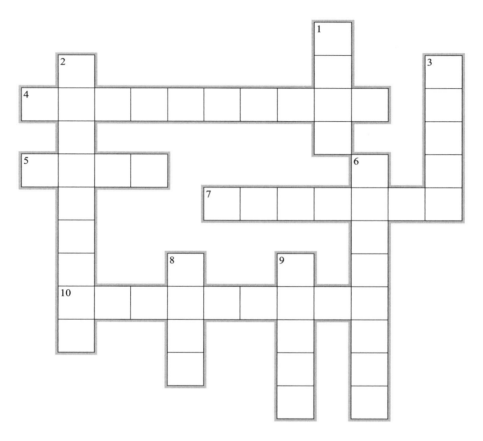

Across
4. peccatum
5. debitum
7. praemium
10. auxilium

Down
1. vallum
2. caelum
3. forum
6. vinum
8. vinum
9. gaudium

Here are some additional derivatives of Latin words in this lesson. Some of them may fit in the crossword. Can you guess which Latin words they come from?

debt   forum   wall

Grammar Crossword

Across

2. a reward (abl.)
4. sins (gen.)
5. joy (gen.)
6. the ramparts (dat.)
9. a sin (nom.)
10. help (acc.)
11. wine (acc.)
12. backs (nom.)
13. heaven (gen.)
15. the forum (abl.)
17. debts (acc.)
18. wine (abl.)
19. rewards (nom.)
20. debt (acc.)
21. aid (abl.)
22. the back (dat.)
23. back (nom.)

Down

1. heaven (nom.)
2. sins (nom.)
3. wine (gen.)
5. joy (abl.)
7. forums (acc.)
8. joys (nom.)
9. the reward (gen.)
11. the rampart (abl.)
13. heaven (abl.)
14. the forums (gen.)
16. the aids (gen.)
17. debts (abl.)
18. ramparts (acc.)

LESSON 13

WORD SEARCH

Find the 10 words (m., f. or n.) of Lesson 13 in the matrix.

```
C  H  X  M  M  Y  C  G  P  T  R  W
F  M  L  U  Q  A  Y  W  M  P  Y  L
J  U  D  T  A  G  L  A  M  R  R  N
Z  L  P  U  T  T  G  U  M  T  G  B
R  T  J  T  N  N  C  N  S  T  J  L
K  A  K  J  U  L  S  N  B  R  Q  F
Y  B  N  M  X  K  U  D  A  Y  T  S
F  H  C  V  P  X  T  Y  J  S  U  M
G  N  F  H  N  Q  L  V  G  V  U  J
S  U  N  E  L  P  A  R  R  N  T  Z
P  M  L  O  N  G  A  A  O  K  J  G
L  T  R  L  Z  H  P  B  M  W  J  L
```

altus, a, um   magnus, a, um
bonus, a, um   plenus, a, um
longus, a, um   sanctus, a, um
malus, a, um   tutus, a, um
multus, a, um   parvus, a, um

54

PARSE STRINGS

plenas	dative singular feminine
malum	dative plural neuter
bonis	genitive plural feminine
altos	accusative plural feminine
tutorum	genitive singular masculine
magnae	accusative plural masculine
parvo	accusative plural neuter
longam	accusative singular masculine
multarum	ablative singular neuter
bonus	genitive plural masculine
sancta	nominative singular masculine
magni	accusative singular feminine

Derivatives Crossword

Complete the crossword using derivatives of the clue words.

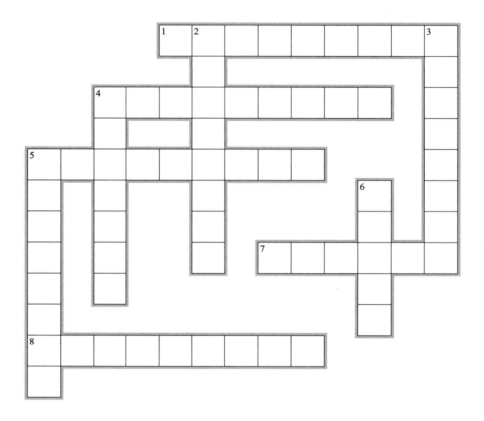

Across
1. malus
4. multus
5. magnus
7. plenus
8. longus

Down
2. altus
3. sanctus
4. magnus
5. multus
6. bonus

Here are some additional derivatives of Latin words in this lesson. Some of them may fit in the crossword. Can you guess which Latin words they come from?

multiplication   malicious   magnitude
sanctity   magnanimous   altimeter

Grammar Crossword

<u>Across</u>

2. much (acc. sing. n.)
4. great (abl. sing. n.)
5. holy (nom. sing. m.)
7. long (nom. sing. n.)
9. full (acc. sing. n.)
11. high (abl. sing. f.)
14. safe (abl. sing. f.)
15. good (gen. sing. n.)
16. great (gen. sing. f.)
18. small (acc. sing. f.)
19. small (dat. sing. f.)
20. good (acc. sing. f.)
22. long (dat. sing. m.)
23. bad (nom. sing. m.)
24. much (nom. sing. f.)
25. bad (abl. sing. f.)

<u>Down</u>

1. bad (abl. sing. m.)
3. safe (acc. sing. n.)
5. holy (dat. sing. f.)
6. holy (acc. sing. f.)
8. much (acc. sing. f.)
10. great (gen. sing. n.)
11. high (dat. sing. n.)
12. safe (gen. sing. m.)
13. long (dat. sing. f.)
17. small (gen. sing. n.)
18. full (abl. sing. n.)
19. full (acc. sing. f.)
20. good (nom. sing. m.)
21. deep (acc. sing. m.)

LESSON 14

WORD SEARCH

Find the 10 words (m., f. or n.) of Lesson 14 in the matrix.

```
T M G M H G S M M N M J
P P U N P U M U Q T S Y
G P R T V C T S Y C E Y
T W B O O R H U R K C N
T E N H E T Z N P N U T
R B R C H X Z R M L N T
A Z B T R R O E W X D M
L F X K I X N T L K U T
O M R T I U P E K Z S B
S U M M U S M A T T R Y
D D A N P R I M A D J R
M T R M K Z Y F H G R Q
```

aeternus, a, um   proximus, a, um
certus, a, um   summus, a, um
primus, a, um   totus, a, um
secundus, a, um   solus, a, um
tertius, a, um   novus, a, um

PARSE STRINGS

certis	genitive plural neuter
summus	accusative plural masculine
primarum	accusative plural feminine
proxima	nominative plural masculine
novos	ablative plural masculine
summas	ablative singular neuter
tertio	nominative plural feminine
aeternorum	nominative singular masculine
novae	accusative singular neuter
primum	genitive plural feminine
secundi	accusative singular feminine
certam	ablative singular feminine

Derivatives Crossword

Complete the crossword using derivatives of the clue words.

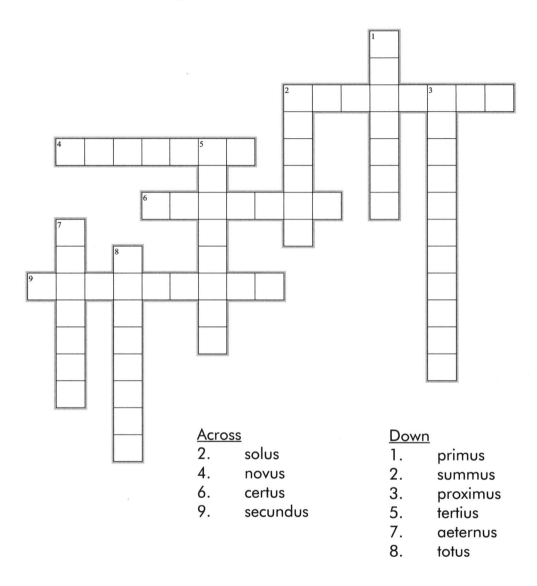

Across
2. solus
4. novus
6. certus
9. secundus

Down
1. primus
2. summus
3. proximus
5. tertius
7. aeternus
8. totus

Here are some additional derivatives of Latin words in this lesson. Some of them may fit in the crossword. Can you guess which Latin words they come from?

eternal	novelty	primal
certain	totality	primordial

Grammar Crossword

Across

1. next (gen. pl. f.)
5. highest (gen. pl. n.)
7. eternal (acc. pl. m.)
10. second (acc. sing. n.)
12. certain (acc. sing. f.)
14. whole (nom. pl. f.)
15. highest (nom. sing. m.)
17. whole (abl. pl. f.)
19. eternal (nom. pl. m.)
20. first (dat. pl. f.)
22. first (gen. pl. f.)
24. new (dat. pl. f.)
27. next (abl. sing. f.)
28. only (acc. pl. f.)

Down

2. eternal (acc. pl. n.)
3. new (nom. pl. f.)
4. next (acc. pl. m.)
6. new (gen. pl. m.)
8. whole (acc. sing. f.)
9. second (nom. pl. f.)
11. certain (abl. sing. m.)
12. certain (gen. pl. n.)
13. third (nom. pl. m.)
16. third (abl. pl. n.)
18. only (abl. sing. m.)
21. second (nom. pl. n.)

22. first (acc. pl. f.)
23. third (dat. sing. n.)
25. highest (nom. pl. n.)
26. alone (abl. sing. f.)

15

LESSON 15

WORD SEARCH

Find the 10 words of Lesson 15 and the forms of the verb possum in the matrix.

```
R P K X S I T S E T O P
I D E W G P O S S U M O
N N O N T T N P Q C K T
T A M P P N O C C N K E
E R R J O S U N L U N S
R P Z R S T U S B N G T
G U W U H M E R S E W G
C S M L Q D C S J O N T
F U W U D M J T B M P E
S R A R A G M T N U K B
H M T L P C F G L C S J
H L C Y A R T N O C L B
```

nunc	numquam	possum
clam	contra	potes
non	sub	potest
bene	supra	possumus
inter	ex	potestis
		possunt

Derivatives Crossword

15

Complete the crossword using derivatives of the clue words.

Across
1. inter
3. possum
5. ex
7. non
9. ex
10. clam
11. ex
13. possum
15. inter
16. bene
17. sub

Down
2. sub
4. contra
6. inter
8. supra
12. bene
14. sub

....

Here are some additional derivatives of Latin words in this lesson. Some of them may fit in the crossword. Can you guess which Latin words they come from?

intervene   possible

exclaim   international

subterranean   interregnum

possibility   export

beneficial   contradiction

....

Grammar Crossword

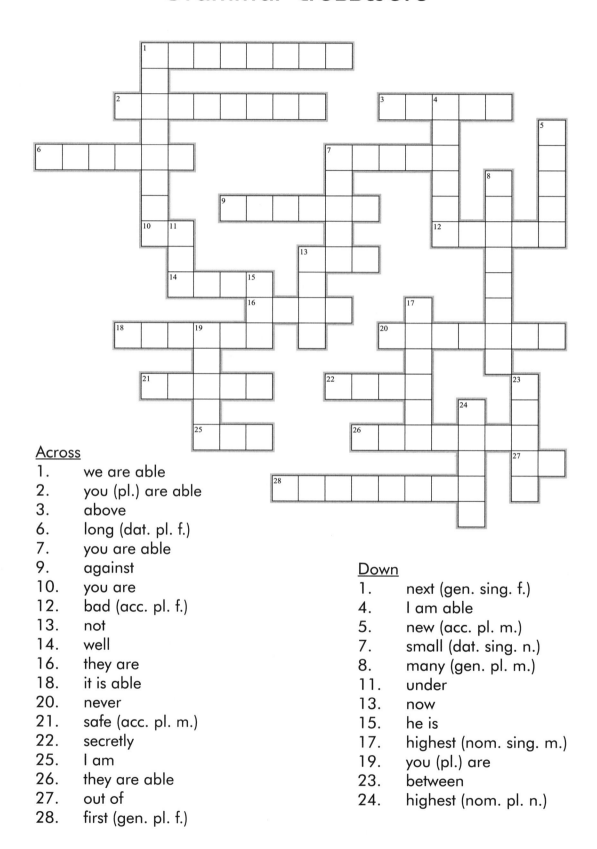

Across
1.   we are able
2.   you (pl.) are able
3.   above
6.   long (dat. pl. f.)
7.   you are able
9.   against
10. you are
12. bad (acc. pl. f.)
13. not
14. well
16. they are
18. it is able
20. never
21. safe (acc. pl. m.)
22. secretly
25. I am
26. they are able
27. out of
28. first (gen. pl. f.)

Down
1.   next (gen. sing. f.)
4.   I am able
5.   new (acc. pl. m.)
7.   small (dat. sing. n.)
8.   many (gen. pl. m.)
11. under
13. now
15. he is
17. highest (nom. sing. m.)
19. you (pl.) are
23. between
24. highest (nom. pl. n.)

Latin Sayings Hangman

_ _ _ _ _ _ _ _ **M** _ _ _ **M**

_ _ _ **L** _ _ _ _

_ _ _ _ **L** **L** _ _ _

_ _ _ _ _ _ _ _ _ _

_ _ _ _ _ _ **D** _ _ _ _ _

D _ _ _ _ _ _ _ _ _ _ _

_ _ _ **U** _ _ _ _ _

_ _ _ _ _ **U** _

LESSON 16

WORD SEARCH

Find the 10 words of Lesson 16 in the matrix.

```
Z  T  H  G  P  J  O  Y  W  D  D  M
W  V  V  A  O  E  C  O  D  F  J  T
F  T  P  C  B  T  E  R  R  E  O  O
K  G  C  U  R  E  X  N  X  Z  E  Z
O  J  J  O  H  L  O  R  T  D  J  T
E  Y  T  E  H  T  J  V  I  F  I  V
B  M  T  N  M  K  Y  V  J  M  P  L
I  M  Z  O  O  G  V  M  E  L  T  N
H  O  X  M  N  E  T  O  N  Y  L  H
O  V  T  T  J  T  B  N  V  J  N  V
R  E  R  N  W  X  L  E  Q  F  Y  V
P  O  T  R  K  J  H  D  D  F  J  R
```

moneo	timeo
video	doceo
terreo	debeo
habeo	prohibeo
moveo	jubeo

PARSE STRINGS

mones	2nd person plural
habet	2nd person singular
jubemus	1st person singular
vident	3rd person singular
timetis	3rd person plural
moveo	1st person plural

Derivatives Crossword

Complete the crossword using derivatives of the clue words.

Across
1. moneo
8. doceo
11. video
12. moveo
13. video

Down
2. moveo
3. habeo
4. debeo
5. moneo
6. terreo
7. prohibeo
9. doceo
10. timeo

Here are some additional derivatives of Latin words in this lesson. Some of them may fit in the crossword. Can you guess which Latin words they come from?

terrify	motor
visual	debit
doctor	prohibition
terrific	automobile
timidity	evidence

Grammar Crossword

Across

1. it moves
4. you fear
5. you move
9. they warn
10. it frightens
12. it prevents
15. we have
17. you owe
19. we move
20. they fear
22. they owe
23. you order
24. we warn
25. they frighten
26. we owe
27. you frighten

Down

2. she sees
3. you (pl.) have
4. he fears
6. I see
7. I teach
8. we prevent
11. you (pl.) teach
13. I order
14. she teaches
15. I have
16. you (pl.) prevent
18. you (pl.) see
21. they order
24. you warn

LESSON 17

WORD SEARCH

Find the 10 words of Lesson 17 in the matrix.

```
A P K A Z K X S U E M L
I K V B P R C A N O F K
R Q D D M P L T E K N Z
U O X L C U E D P P A K
J J M B S F E L T D R K
N J P N U S H T L K R T
I T I T N P Q M Y O O F
M D J K G R T B M W K X
M V Y S A L T Q J R T X
R X M P U O C U L U S K
T Q K W Q U C Z B D G K
Y K R C P T T J Z N K F
```

agnus	do
insula	meus, a, um
oculus	tuus, a, um
appello	injuria
narro	sedeo

PARSE STRINGS

sedemus	dative plural
narrant	2nd person plural
agnos	genitive singular
oculum	3rd person plural
mea	2nd person singular
meis	accusative plural
do	genitive plural
insulae	accusative singular
docetis	1st person plural
tuo	dative singular
appellas	1st person singular
timet	ablative singular
injuriarum	3rd person singular

17

Derivatives Crossword

Complete the crossword using derivatives of the clue words.

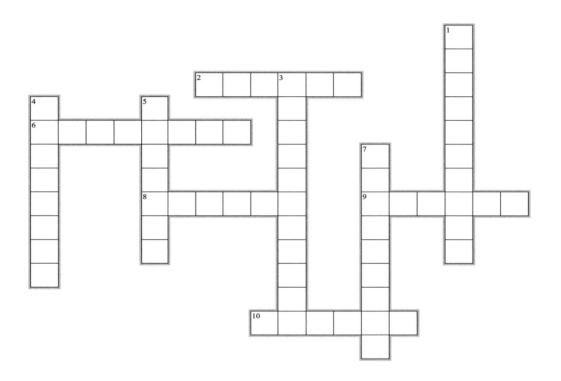

Across		Down	
2.	sedeo	1.	oculus
6.	narro	3.	appello
8.	appello	4.	insula
9.	do	5.	narro
10.	injuria	7.	sedeo

Here are some additional derivatives of Latin words in this lesson. Some of them may fit in the crossword. Can you guess which Latin words they come from?

binoculars   injury   narrative

Grammatical Forms Crossword

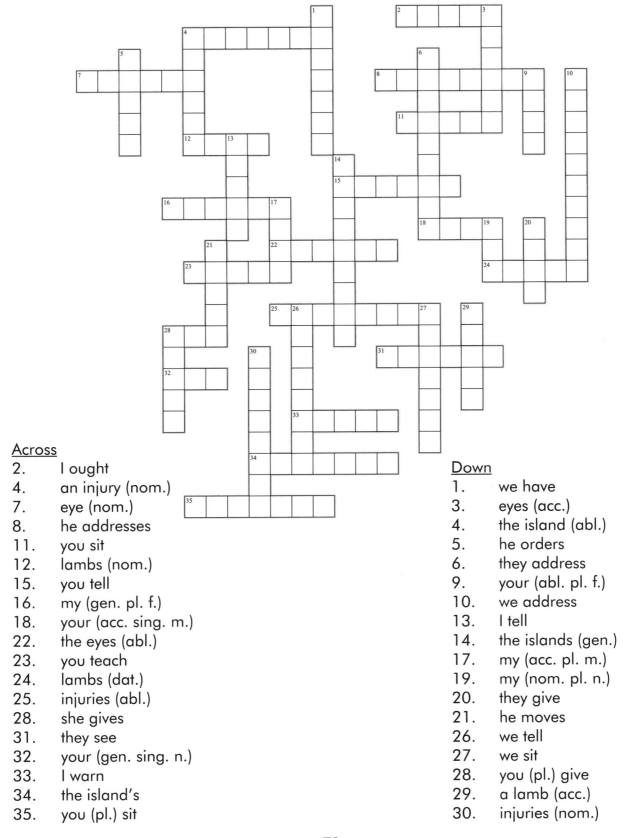

Across

2. I ought
4. an injury (nom.)
7. eye (nom.)
8. he addresses
11. you sit
12. lambs (nom.)
15. you tell
16. my (gen. pl. f.)
18. your (acc. sing. m.)
22. the eyes (abl.)
23. you teach
24. lambs (dat.)
25. injuries (abl.)
28. she gives
31. they see
32. your (gen. sing. n.)
33. I warn
34. the island's
35. you (pl.) sit

Down

1. we have
3. eyes (acc.)
4. the island (abl.)
5. he orders
6. they address
9. your (abl. pl. f.)
10. we address
13. I tell
14. the islands (gen.)
17. my (acc. pl. m.)
19. my (nom. pl. n.)
20. they give
21. he moves
26. we tell
27. we sit
28. you (pl.) give
29. a lamb (acc.)
30. injuries (nom.)

18-19

LESSONS 18 - 19

WORD SEARCH

Find the words of Lesson 18 in the matrix.

```
N N B P Z T H R G Y D Y
S A M A L Z Y R V G B L
U N R R U K T A R K M A
T Q Y T W R N B S N S V
R Y K O S E I I H U N O
O Y Q T C E C G B X G C
H T X I B U N M A R L Y
F M B B T F I E W H C B
K G J A N N P R F N Q J
L D L H P A U R O R A R
A N G U P L M R T R T Z
G W Y G M G M B H N G Y
```

habito   sicut
cena   pugna
aurora   fenestra
auriga   hortus
lavo   nimbus

WORD SEARCH

Find the words of Lesson 19 in the matrix.

```
L A R N W F N F T P X S
Z Q C R B P S J K A J U
D U Z A R D H U R F P I
K A W W P N K B R I L R
Z R R V O R I R S U N A
S I E D G L I C N B A T
U U C R R M E C K W T T
N S N B I S V C O T Y I
I Z A V V W V R R T G
M R C O S E I R A P N A
E R E B R T Q L J P Q S
G L F S C O R P I O Y F
```

virgo
libra
scorpio
sagittarius
capricorn
aquarius

pisces
aries
taurus
geminus
cancer
leo

PARSE STRINGS

lavabis	2nd person singular present
pugnat	3rd person plural future
narrabimus	1st person singular future
laboramus	1st person singular present
dabunt	3rd person singular present
appello	1st person plural present
habitatis	3rd person plural present
vocabit	2nd person singular future
judicabo	3rd person singular future
laudabitis	1st person plural future
ambulas	2nd person plural future
portant	2nd person plural present

Derivatives Crossword

Complete the crossword using derivatives of the clue words from Lesson 18 and the names of the constellations from Lesson 19.

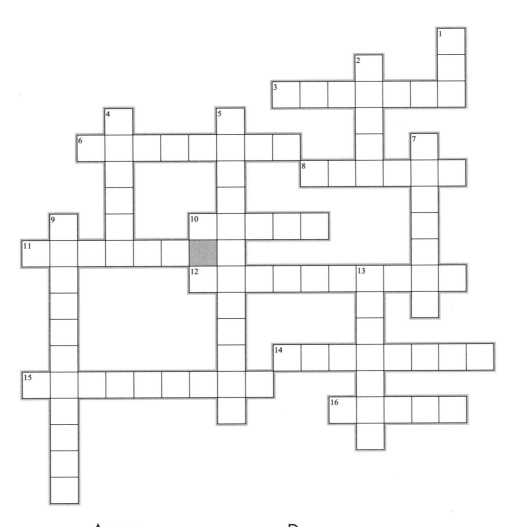

Across		Down	
3.	Scorpion	1.	Lion
6.	lavo	2.	Ram
8.	Fish	4.	Crab
10.	Scales	5.	hortus
11.	Bull	7.	Twin
12.	pugna	9.	Archer
14.	Water Carrier	13.	habito
15.	Goat		
16.	Virgin		

LESSON 20

WORD SEARCH

Find the 10 words of Lesson 20 in the matrix.

```
M  M  L  L  D  L  Z  Q  P  T  T  R
L  M  W  B  F  R  R  T  W  F  E  N
R  R  M  P  Q  E  E  T  T  T  R  S
R  N  C  X  P  X  T  J  A  T  X  U
N  Q  X  L  M  E  A  P  R  L  P  M
A  R  K  J  E  K  R  M  Y  E  Q  I
R  U  P  J  X  X  F  J  C  Z  H  X
M  T  G  R  C  H  P  U  R  L  W  O
M  R  P  N  L  L  N  M  A  T  E  R
T  H  L  Q  I  I  L  G  P  M  M  P
Q  F  Z  C  A  L  X  G  G  J  W  R
K  K  G  R  A  S  N  E  M  M  W  Q
```

frater	pecunia
pater	mensa
mater	lingua
lex	proximus
rex	et

PARSE STRINGS

movebo	1st person singular present
jubes	2nd person plural present
prohibeo	3rd person singular present
vident	1st person singular future
sedebimus	2nd person plural future
terrebis	2nd person singular present
habet	3rd person plural future
docebitis	2nd person singular future
timemus	1st person plural present
debebit	3rd person plural present
monetis	3rd person singular future
jubebunt	1st person plural future

Derivatives Crossword

Complete the crossword using derivatives of the clue words.

Across
4. pater, patris
6. proximus
8. lex, legis
9. rex, regis
11. mater, matris
12. pater, patris
13. frater, fratris

Down
1. frater, fratris
2. pecunia
3. lingua
5. lex, legis
7. mensa
10. et

Here are some additional derivatives of Latin words in this lesson. Some of them may fit in the crossword. Can you guess which Latin words they come from?

language	pecuniary
mesa	maternity
proximity	patriot
etcetera	legality

Grammar Crossword

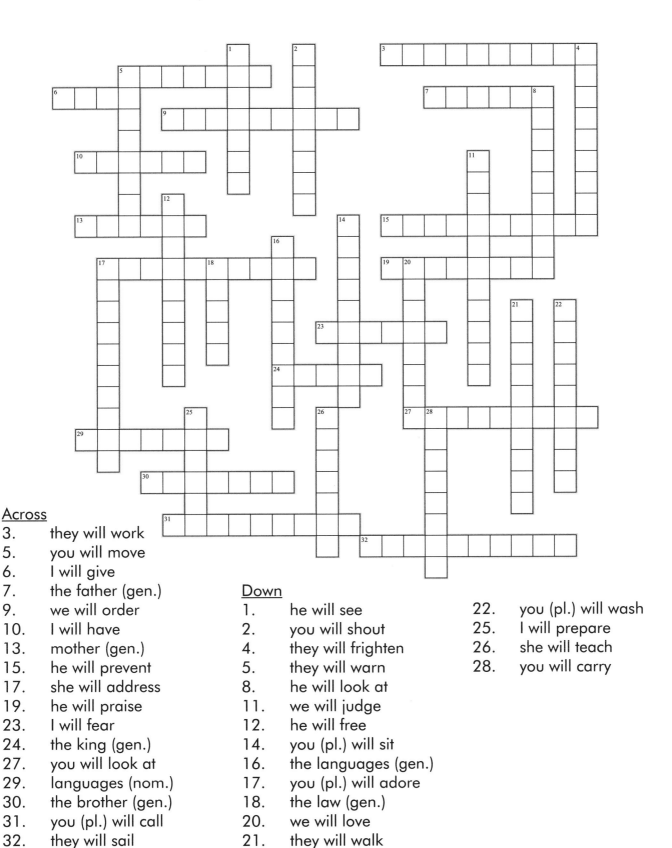

Across

3. they will work
5. you will move
6. I will give
7. the father (gen.)
9. we will order
10. I will have
13. mother (gen.)
15. he will prevent
17. she will address
19. he will praise
23. I will fear
24. the king (gen.)
27. you will look at
29. languages (nom.)
30. the brother (gen.)
31. you (pl.) will call
32. they will sail

Down

1. he will see
2. you will shout
4. they will frighten
5. they will warn
8. he will look at
11. we will judge
12. he will free
14. you (pl.) will sit
16. the languages (gen.)
17. you (pl.) will adore
18. the law (gen.)
20. we will love
21. they will walk

22. you (pl.) will wash
25. I will prepare
26. she will teach
28. you will carry

Latin Sayings Hangman

_ _ _ _ _ _ _ _ _ _ _ _ _ _ _

_ _ _ _ A _ _ _ _ _ A

_ _ M _ M _ _ _ _ _

_ _ _ _ _ _ _ _ _ _ _ _ _ _ _ _ _ _ _ _

_ _ C C _ _ _ _ _ _ _

_ E _ _ _ D _ _ _ _ _ _

_ _ O _ A _ _ _

LESSONS 21-22

WORD SEARCH

Find the words of Lesson 21 in the matrix.

```
W B P S R Q H T M D W R
P K M U X J R Q C T F S
K T G P U K D A T H A S
N W X M L Z P L R T I R
L V R E F U Q B I N N Y
O M M T T X V R G R Q R
H D P T Y G E I M D T Z
P V R Y R V R P T Z H F
Z O N O K D T A B M F N
X J N M Y M P X Y K Y N
Q K Z S S I T S O H Q T
K C A E S A R N X M K R
```

lux   caput
veritas   hostis
Caesar   ordo
pons   tempus
pax   ignis

21-22

WORD SEARCH

Find the words of Lesson 22 in the matrix.

```
C N X M N T T T M L D Y
R O N R D L R O R O S G
M G R N W M Y J A H H K
O X N P K C F L P R Z X
I J O S U Z D M N T O K
R W M E V S Y K Z S Z H
U N E L X B D C A N I S
T L N I L X V T R V N W
N C K M J Q I Z C O Q F
E J D L M V W T M X A Y
C N R H I K Y Y T M M Q
K T L C C K F M A V T L
```

miles	fama
mons	soror
canis	hora
corpus	centurio
nomen	civitas

PARSE STRINGS

vocabat	2nd person singular future
portant	1st person plural imperfect
orabunt	1st person singular imperfect
laborabam	2nd person plural imperfect
judicabant	3rd person singular imperfect
narrabo	1st person plural future
appellabis	3rd person plural future
ambulabas	1st person plural present
amabimus	3rd person plural present
pugnabamus	3rd person plural imperfect
navigamus	2nd person singular imperfect
clamabatis	1st person singular future

21-22

Derivatives Crossword

Complete the crossword using derivatives of the clue words.

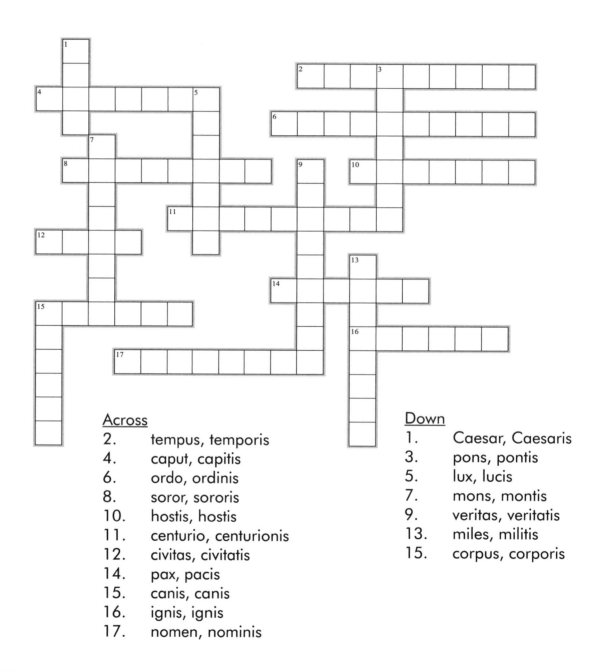

Across
2. tempus, temporis
4. caput, capitis
6. ordo, ordinis
8. soror, sororis
10. hostis, hostis
11. centurio, centurionis
12. civitas, civitatis
14. pax, pacis
15. canis, canis
16. ignis, ignis
17. nomen, nominis

Down
1. Caesar, Caesaris
3. pons, pontis
5. lux, lucis
7. mons, montis
9. veritas, veritatis
13. miles, militis
15. corpus, corporis

Here are some additional derivatives of Latin words in this lesson. Some of them may fit in the crossword. Can you guess which Latin words they come from?

czar   mountain   centurion
ordination   veritable   militarize

Grammar Crossword

Across

3. light (nom.)
4. mountain (nom.)
7. the head (gen.)
10. fire (gen.)
12. the body (gen.)
13. state (nom.)
16. the state (gen.)
18. time (nom.)
19. a dog (gen.)
20. body (nom.)
22. the name (gen.)
23. a soldier (nom.)
26. peace (nom.)
27. the centurion (gen.)
30. Caesar (nom.)
31. a rank (gen.)

Down

1. the truth (gen.)
2. the mountain (gen.)
3. the light (gen.)
5. the sister (gen.)
6. centurion (nom.)
8. peace (gen.)
9. bridge (nom.)
11. the bridge (gen.)
14. the time (gen.)
15. Caesar (gen.)
16. head (nom.)
17. truth (nom.)
21. the enemy (gen.)

24. sister (nom.)
25. the soldier (gen.)
28. name (nom.)
29. rank (nom.)

LESSON 23

WORD SEARCH

Find the 10 words of Lesson 23 in the matrix.

```
Y J R F Z C L J F D H K
X T N Z N P K V G A N K
I T D J P M T Z V T R B
M H U K F V R L K A X X
P K O C Z F I G U O G M
E X R M I S P R V M B K
R D S Y O S I B K S G X
A N U Y R G A R I B T L
T N T D A X T T G R Y T
O Q O T N T L Z M U K B
R B T N D L E G I O B L
W B Y T V Y M X W Z K T
```

urbs	auriga
vox	ira
legio	sicut
homo	totus, a, um
imperator	silva

PARSE STRINGS

sedebatis	1st person plural present
videmus	2nd person singular imperfect
jubebitis	2nd person plural future
habes	3rd person plural future
docebat	3rd person plural imperfect
terrebam	2nd person singular present
monebunt	2nd person plural imperfect
videbas	1st person singular future
movebimus	1st person singular imperfect
habebamus	1st person plural imperfect
docebant	3rd person singular imperfect
movebo	1st person plural future

23

Derivatives Crossword

Complete the crossword using derivatives of the clue words.

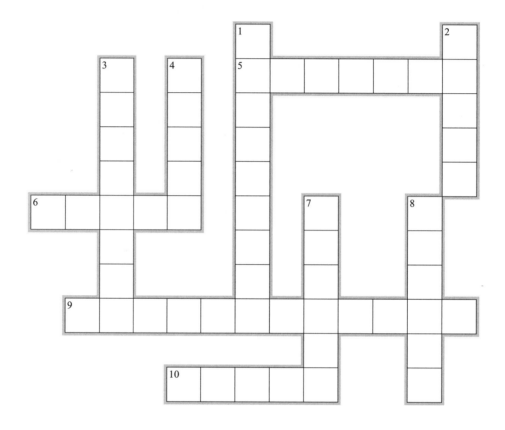

Across
5.   imperator, imperatoris
6.   vox, vocis
9.   silva
10.   urbs, urbis

Down
1.   legio, legionis
2.   ira
3.   homo, hominis
4.   totus
7.   silva
8.   legio, legionis

Here are some additional derivatives of Latin words in this lesson. Some of them may fit in the crossword. Can you guess which Latin words they come from?

total   legion   emperor
sylvan   Pennsylvania   corps

Grammar Crossword

Across

5.   I was praising
8.   of the voice
11. he was sailing
12. he was washing
13. you were giving
15. man
17. I was having
18. anger (direct object)
23. I was shouting
25. voice
26. legion
27. you were looking at
29. you (pl.) were moving
31. they were praying
32. you (pl.) were carrying
33. you were seeing

Down

1.   the commander's
2.   she was walking
3.   they were frightening
4.   charioteers (subject)
6.   she was teaching
7.   a man's
9.   they were ordering
10. we were working
14. the legion's
16. I was sitting
19. of the forests
20. you (pl.) were fighting
21. it was preventing
22. commander
24. you were warning
25. they were calling
28. of the city
30. all (dat. pl. f.)

24-25

LESSONS 24-25

WORD SEARCH

Find the words of Lesson 24 in the matrix.

```
J  M  J  G  Q  T  G  M  S  D  N  K
X  F  R  M  U  L  A  U  B  C  V  J
S  B  L  T  Z  X  I  P  N  T  G  R
U  T  U  L  H  T  R  N  K  O  R  R
T  S  P  M  N  H  T  X  R  M  X  B
R  B  Y  U  U  F  A  Q  S  M  H  F
I  D  N  Q  T  I  P  I  C  J  C  H
V  N  A  V  I  S  L  M  N  M  R  M
P  W  W  C  K  L  K  E  T  R  U  F
G  Z  W  W  O  B  L  M  O  Q  X  J
K  D  P  C  X  N  V  J  R  R  K  H
L  M  U  I  M  E  A  R  P  M  P  R
```

virtus	tutus, a, um
collis	praemium
navis	proelium
nox	patria
crux	nuntius

WORD SEARCH

Find the words of Lesson 25 in the matrix.

```
L K X B X S L R Z N L H
P O Q M N L L M Y V G J
D T F E G H B J N X K O
R K G L O Z K X G K C R
O W M D U T K J Z N J R
L R O Q H M I M L R G A
O X R R V Y E B L B V N
D L S N L X H N A R Z Q
R F P A R S C M T H T K
R K V O L L E P P A K B
B O M R F L Q M N J V N
V C Z K Z T P Z K T F D
```

dolor
gens
pars
flumen
mors

lavo
appello
habito
narro
do

24-25

PARSE STRINGS

nobis	accusative plural
te	dative plural
mihi	nominative singular
vos	dative singular
vestrum	genitive singular
tui	genitive plural
ego	ablative singular

Derivatives Crossword

Complete the crossword using derivatives of the clue words.

Across
2. habito
6. crux, crucis
9. nuntius
13. virtus, virtutis
15. mors, mortis
16. lavo
17. dolor, doloris
18. do

Down
1. narro
3. navis, navis
4. crux, crucis
5. praemium
7. gens, gentis
8. pars, partis
10. nox, noctis
11. appello
12. patria
14. flumen, fluminis

Here are some additional derivatives of Latin words in this lesson. Some of them may fit in the crossword. Can you guess which Latin words they come from?

narration	lavatory
donation	patriotism
habitation	part
annunciation	generation
appeal	premium

Grammar Crossword

24-25

Across

4. in/by/with/from battles
7. night
9. the river's
12. virtue
13. to/for us
14. part
15. to/for you
18. of you
19. rewards (subject)
22. I (subject)
24. of the hill
25. of the night
27. of us
30. in/by/with/from you (pl.)
31. of you (pl.)
33. safe (nom. sing. n.)
34. we (subject)
35. to/for me

Down

1. cross
2. in/by/with/from you
3. of virtue
5. the tribe's
6. you (pl., direct object)
7. messengers (subject)
8. of sorrow
10. of us
11. of the fatherland
16. of the cross
17. tribe
18. you (subject)
20. of death
21. sorrow
23. death
26. river
27. the ship's
28. safe (acc. pl. n.)
29. of the part
30. of you (pl.)
32. of me
35. me (direct object)

Latin Sayings Hangman

_ _ _ E _ _ _ _ _ _ _ _
_ U _

_ _ X _ _ _ _ _ _ _ X _ _ _ _ _

E _ _ _ _ _ _ _ E

_ _ _ N _ M _ _ _ _ _ _ _

_ _ _ _ _ O M _ _ _

Group Games

Gladiators

For 2 teams.
Teams form into 2 lines facing one another. Players in turn "duel" by competing to be the first to correctly answer a question given by the teacher.
The winner is the first team to get a set number of points.

Josho

For 2 players or teams.
Each player thinks of a word, which is kept secret.
One player submits a test word to the other, who responds by saying which letters are in his or her secret word.
Then the other side submits a test word, and so on.
The player wins who guesses the other's word first.
[More difficult: players respond only with how many letters coincide, not which letters.]

Memory

For groups of players.
The players are shown a word, which is then concealed.
Then they are show that word again with a second word, and so on.
The player wins who can remember the longest string of words.
[More difficult: new words are shown without the previous words.]

Jeopardy-Bingo

For 2 teams.
Mark off the board into categories, such as derivatives, history, grammar, vocabulary, sayings. Play the TV game or give extra points for correct answers in a vertical, horizontal or diagonal row.
Teams can be given names such as Romani et Graeci (or Barbari, Galli, etc.) or Pueri et Puellae.

Pictionary

For 2 teams.
A student is given a Latin word which he must illustrate on the blackboard with a picture. His or her teammates try to guess the word for points.
The winner is the team with the most points.

ANSWER KEYS

Lesson 1

Derivatives

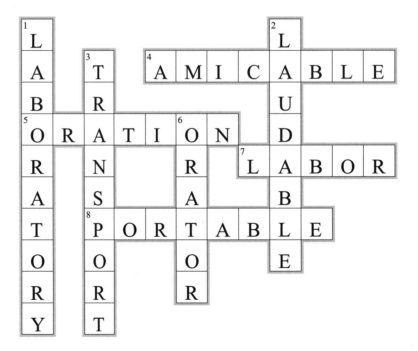

Lesson 2

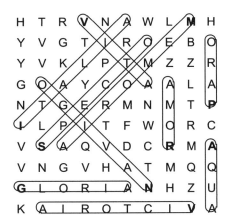

```
H  T  R  V  N  A  W  L  M  H
Y  V  G  T  I  R  O  E  B  O
Y  V  K  L  P  T  M  Z  Z  R
G  O  A  Y  C  O  A  L  A
N  T  G  E  R  M  N  M  T  P
I  L  P  I  T  F  W  O  R  C
V  S  A  Q  V  D  C  R  M  A
V  N  G  V  H  A  T  M  Q  Q
G  L  O  R  I  A  N  H  Z  U
K  A  I  R  O  T  C  I  V  A
```

PARSE STRINGS

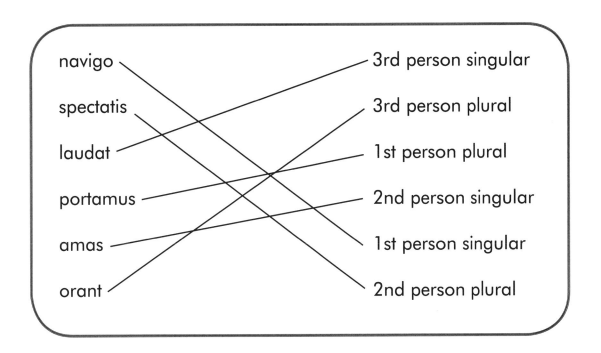

navigo — 3rd person singular

spectatis — 3rd person plural

laudat — 1st person plural

portamus — 2nd person singular

amas — 1st person singular

orant — 2nd person plural

Derivatives

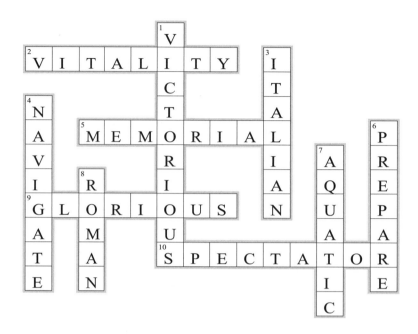

Grammar

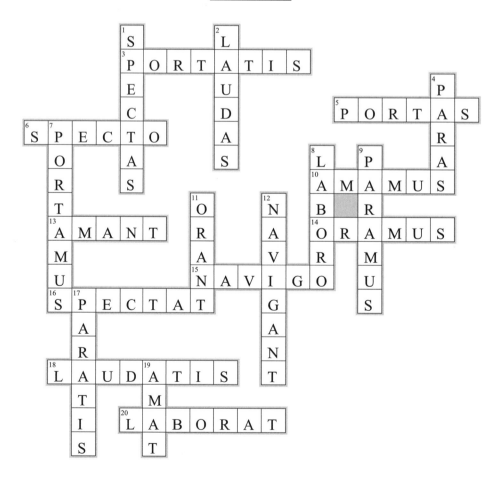

Lesson 3

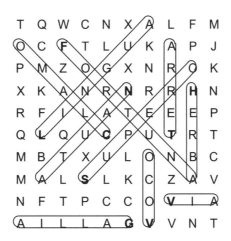

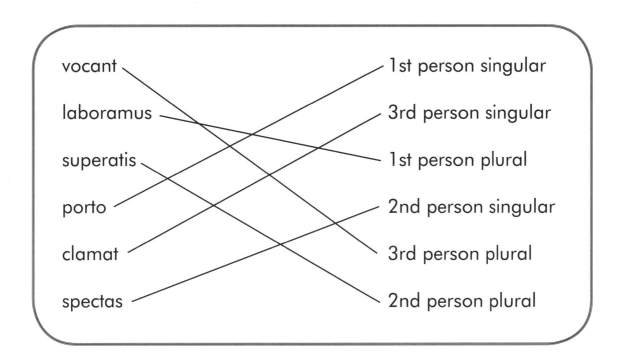

vocant — 1st person singular
laboramus — 3rd person singular
superatis — 1st person plural
porto — 2nd person singular
clamat — 3rd person plural
spectas — 2nd person plural

Derivatives

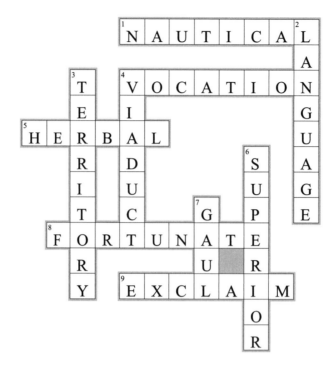

Grammar

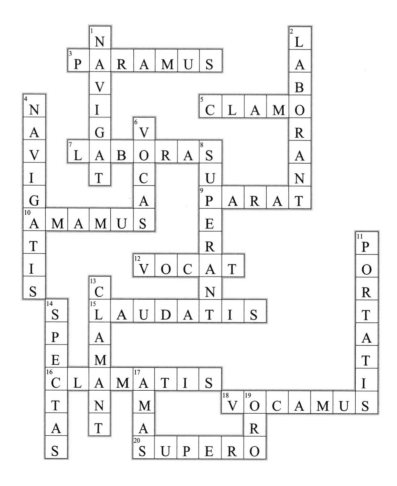

Lesson 4

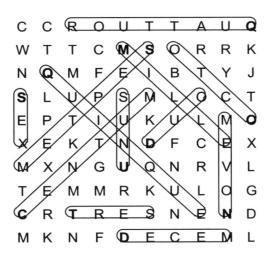

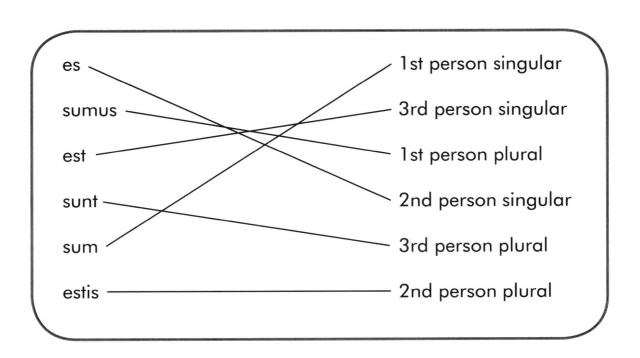

Derivatives

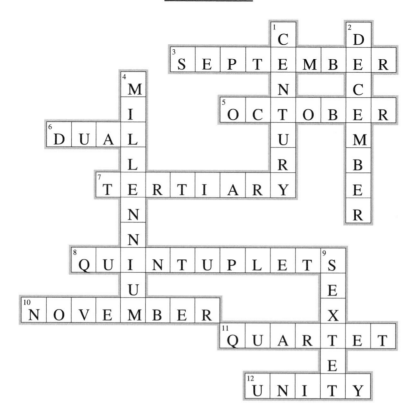

Grammar

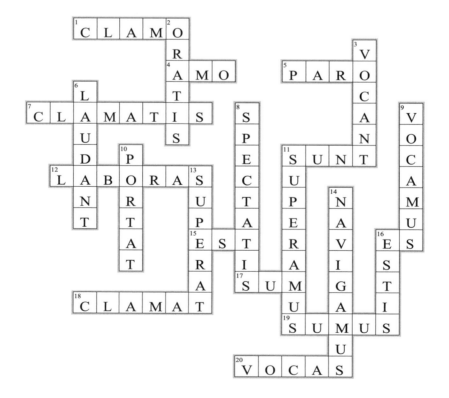

Lesson 5

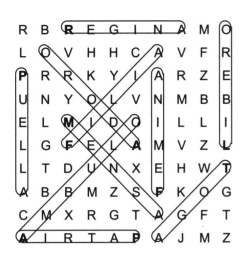

Derivatives

Grammar

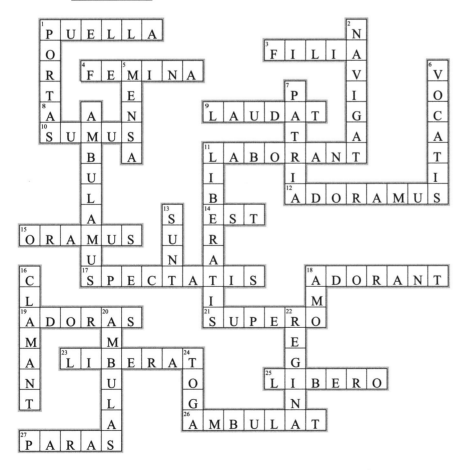

Hangman Lessons 1-5

E PLURIBUS UNUM
LABOR OMNIA VINCIT
MATER ITALIAE ROMA
CAELUM ET TERRA
ORA ET LABORA

Lesson 6

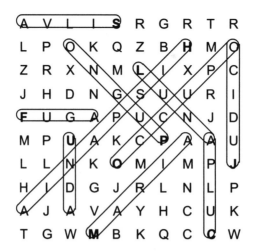

PARSE STRINGS

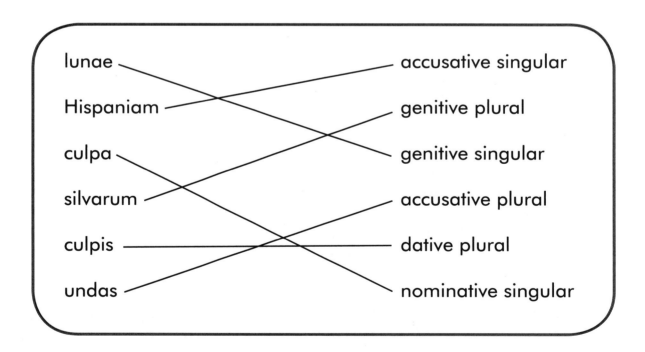

Derivatives

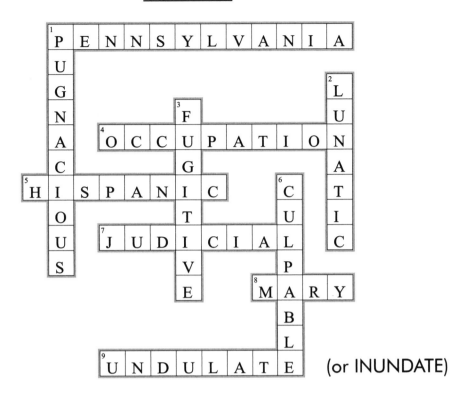

(or INUNDATE)

Grammar

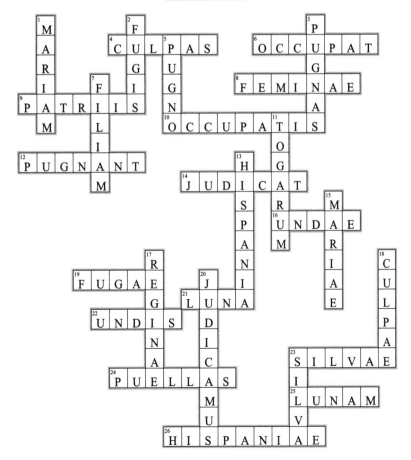

Lesson 7

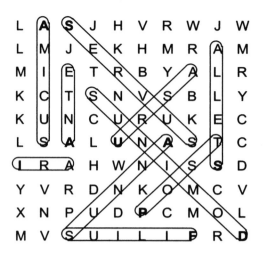

```
L  A  S  J  H  V  R  W  J  W
L  M  J  E  K  H  M  R  A  M
M  I  E  T  R  B  Y  A  L  R
K  C  T  S  N  V  S  B  L  Y
K  U  N  C  U  R  U  K  E  C
L  S  A  L  U  N  A  S  T  C
I  R  A  H  W  N  I  S  S  D
Y  V  R  D  N  K  O  M  C  V
X  N  P  U  D  P  C  M  O  L
M  V  S  U  I  L  I  P  R  D
```

PARSE STRINGS

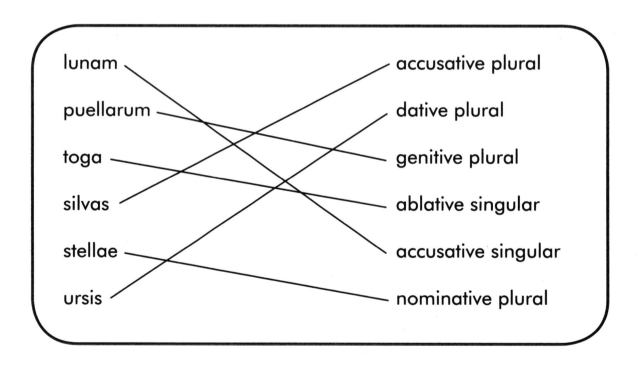

lunam — accusative plural

puellarum — dative plural

toga — genitive plural

silvas — ablative singular

stellae — accusative singular

ursis — nominative plural

Derivatives

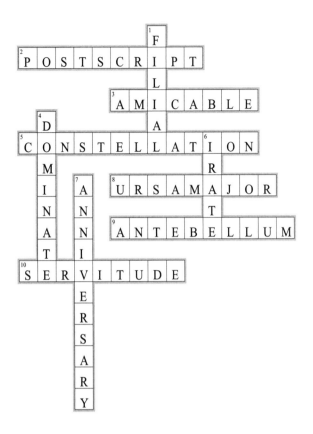

2 POSTSCRIPT

1 F

3 AMICABLE

5 CONSTELLATION

8 URSA MAJOR

9 ANTEBELLUM

10 SERVITUDE

Grammar

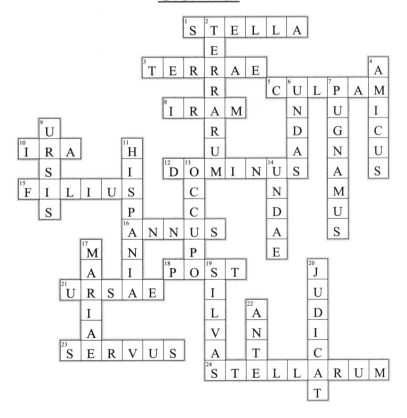

1 S **2** STELLA

3 TERRAE

5 CULPAM

8 IRAM

10 IRA

15 FILIUS

12 DOMINUS

16 ANNUS

18 POST

21 URSAE

23 SERVUS

24 STELLARUM

Lesson 8

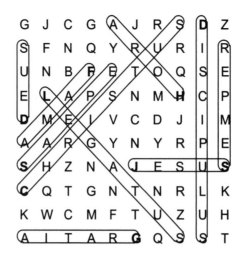

```
G J C G A J R S D Z
S F N Q Y R U R I R
U N B F E T O Q S E
E L A P S N M H C P
D M E I V C D J I M
A A R G Y N Y R P E
S H Z N A J E S U S
C Q T G N T N R L K
K W C M F T U Z U H
A I T A R G Q S S T
```

PARSE   STRINGS

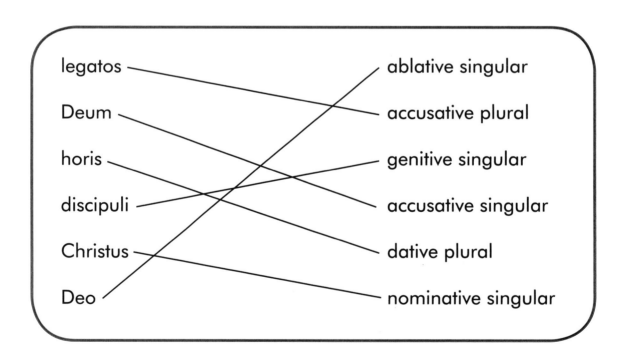

legatos — accusative plural

Deum — accusative singular

horis — dative plural

discipuli — nominative singular

Christus — nominative singular

Deo — ablative singular

legatos — ablative singular
Deum — accusative plural
horis — genitive singular
discipuli — accusative singular
Christus — dative plural
Deo — nominative singular

114

Derivatives

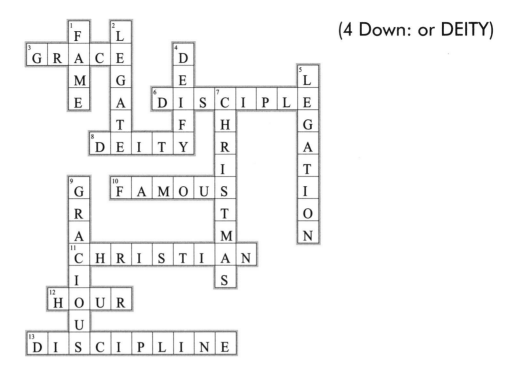

(4 Down: or DEITY)

Grammar

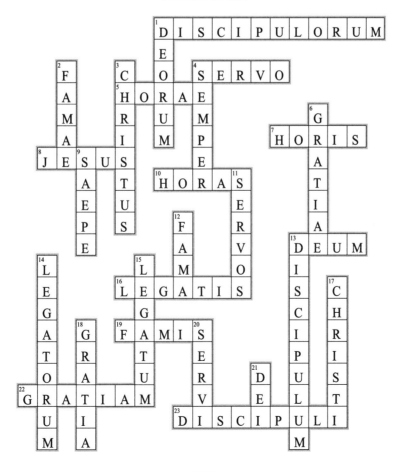

Lesson 9

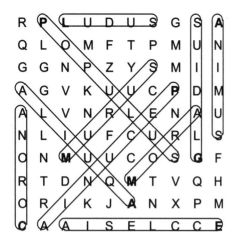

PARSE STRINGS

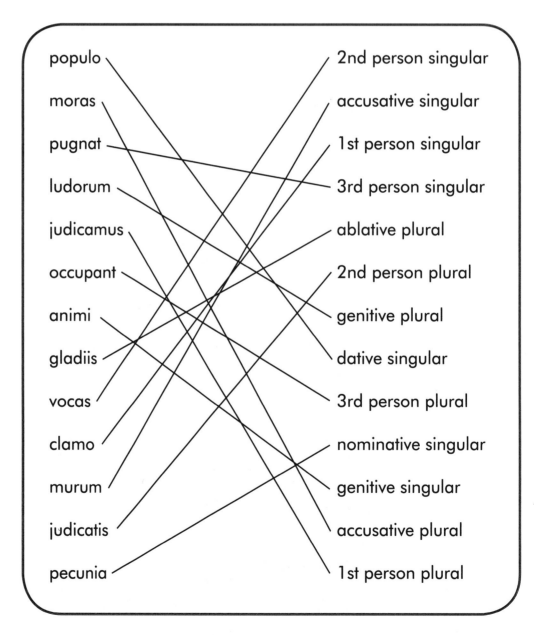

populo

moras

pugnat

ludorum

judicamus

occupant

animi

gladiis

vocas

clamo

murum

judicatis

pecunia

2nd person singular

accusative singular

1st person singular

3rd person singular

ablative plural

2nd person plural

genitive plural

dative singular

3rd person plural

nominative singular

genitive singular

accusative plural

1st person plural

Derivatives

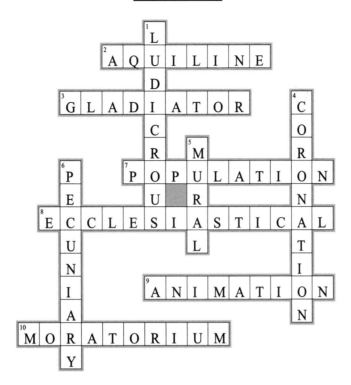

Grammar

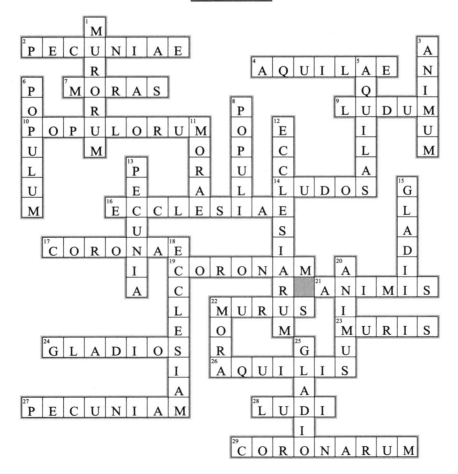

Lesson 10

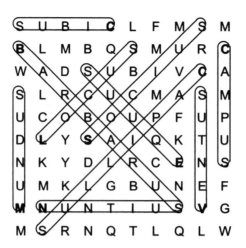

PARSE STRINGS

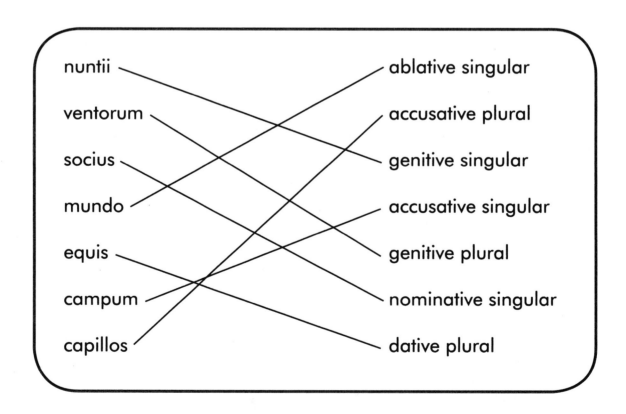

nuntii — accusative plural

ventorum — genitive plural

socius — nominative singular

mundo — ablative singular

equis — dative plural

campum — accusative singular

capillos — genitive singular

Derivatives

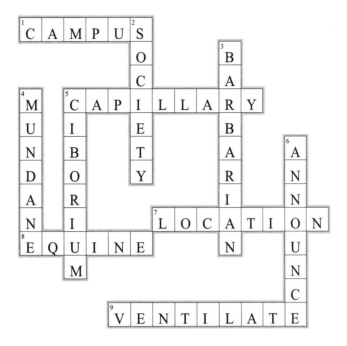

Grammar

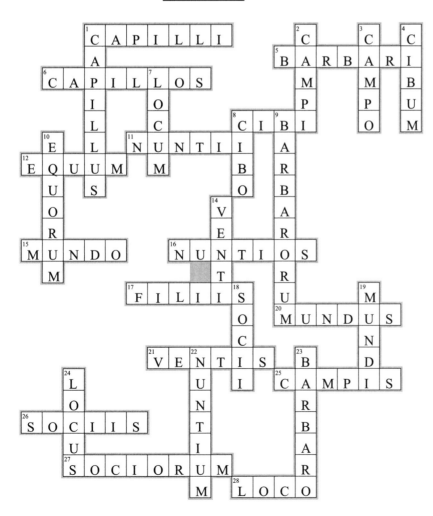

Hangman Lessons 6-10

ANNO DOMINI
SENATUS POPULUSQUE
ROMANUS
STUPOR MUNDI
MEA CULPA
SEMPER FIDELIS

Lesson 11

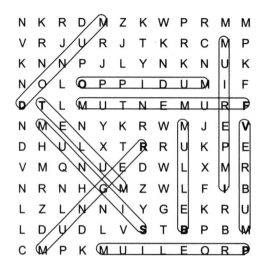

```
N K R D M Z K W P R M M
V R J U R J T K R C M P
K N N P J L Y N K N U K
N O L O P P I D U M I F
D T L M U T N E M U R P
N M E N Y K R W M J E V
D H U L X T R R U K P E
V M Q N U E D W L X M R
N R N H G M Z W L F U B
L Z L N I Y G E K R U
L D U D L V S T B P B M
C M P K M U I L E O R P
```

PARSE STRINGS

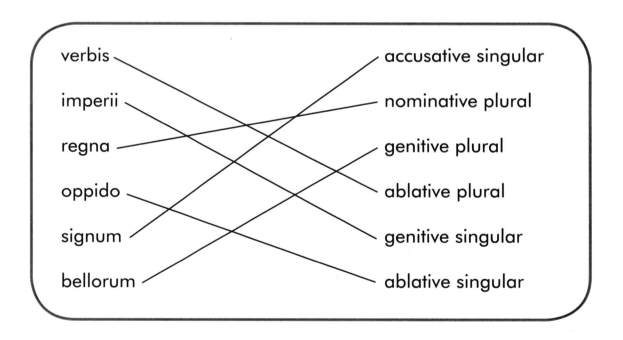

verbis — accusative singular

imperii — nominative plural

regna — genitive plural

oppido — ablative plural

signum — genitive singular

bellorum — ablative singular

Derivatives

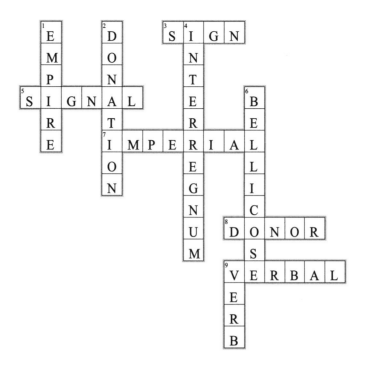

Grammar

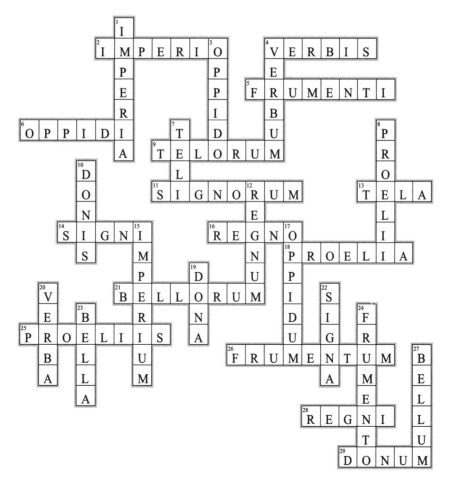

Lesson 12

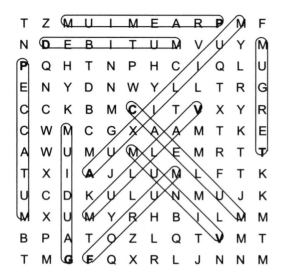

PARSE STRINGS

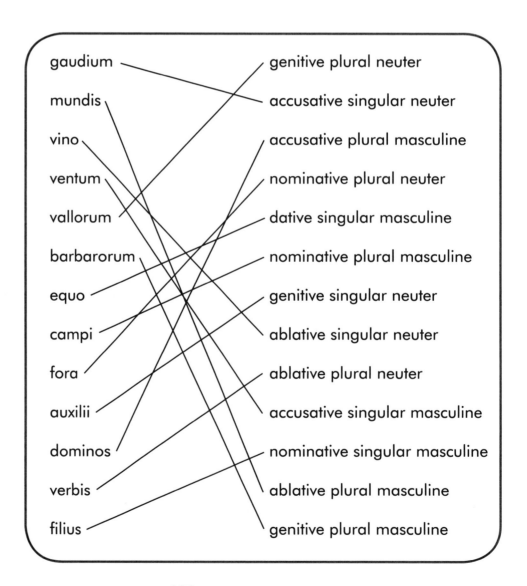

gaudium — genitive plural neuter

mundis — accusative singular neuter

vino — accusative plural masculine

ventum — nominative plural neuter

vallorum — dative singular masculine

barbarorum — nominative plural masculine

equo — genitive singular neuter

campi — ablative singular neuter

fora — ablative plural neuter

auxilii — accusative singular masculine

dominos — nominative singular masculine

verbis — ablative plural masculine

filius — genitive plural masculine

Derivatives

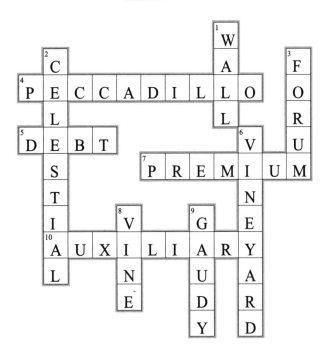

Grammar

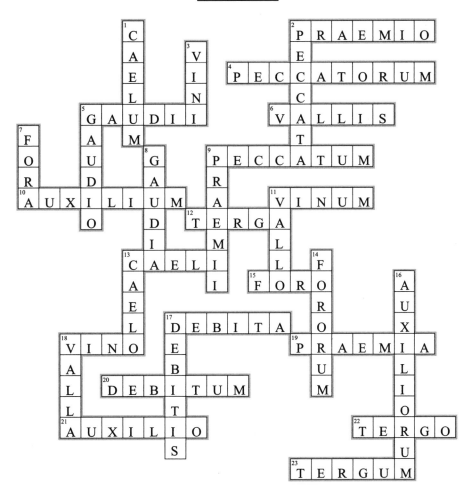

Lesson 13

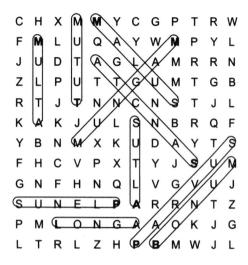

```
C H X M W Y C G P T R W
F M L U Q A Y W M P Y L
J U D T A G L A M R R N
Z L P U T T G U M T G B
R T J T N C N S T J L
K A K J U L S N B R Q F
Y B N W X K U D A Y T S
F H C V P X T Y J S U M
G N F H N Q L V G V U J
S U N E L P A R R N T Z
P M L O N G A A O K J G
L T R L Z H P B M W J L
```

PARSE STRINGS

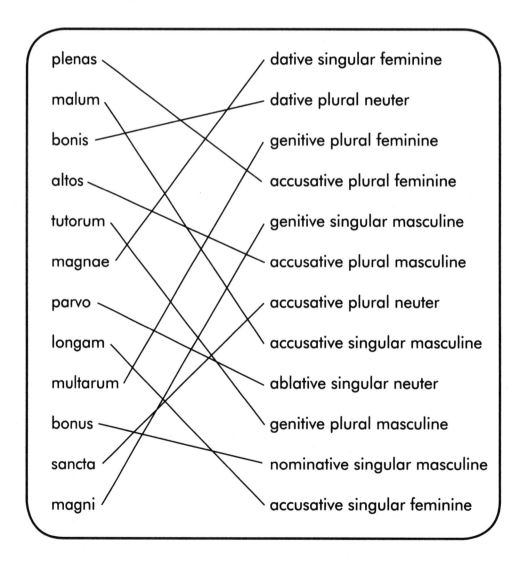

plenas — dative singular feminine

malum — dative plural neuter

bonis — genitive plural feminine

altos — accusative plural feminine

tutorum — genitive singular masculine

magnae — accusative plural masculine

parvo — accusative plural neuter

longam — accusative singular masculine

multarum — ablative singular neuter

bonus — genitive plural masculine

sancta — nominative singular masculine

magni — accusative singular feminine

Derivatives

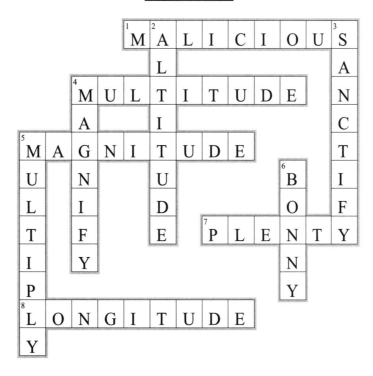

Grammar

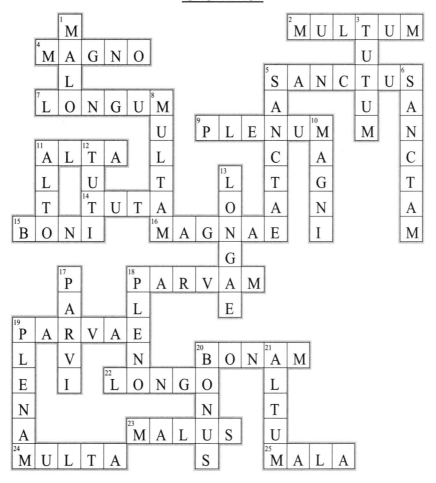

Lesson 14

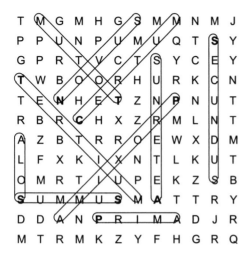

PARSE STRINGS

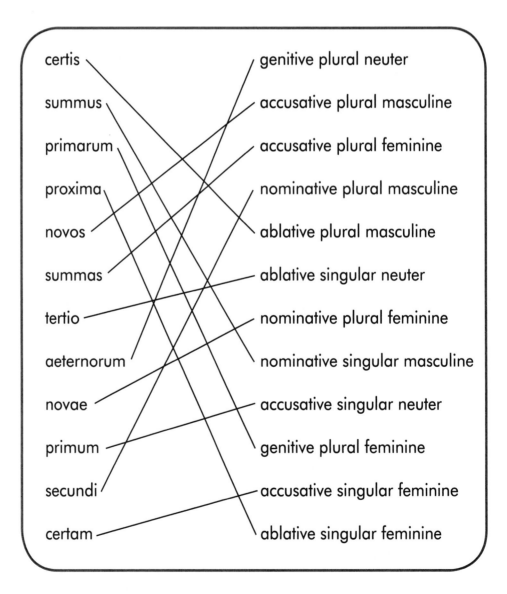

Derivatives

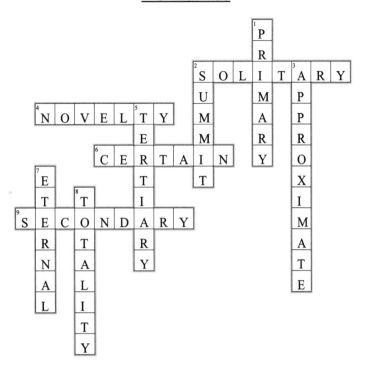

Grammar

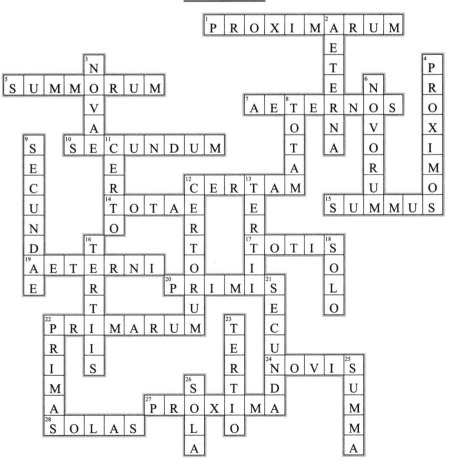

Lesson 15

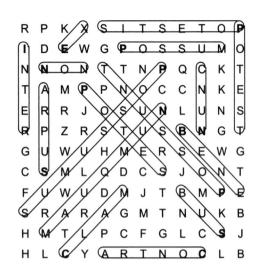

Derivatives

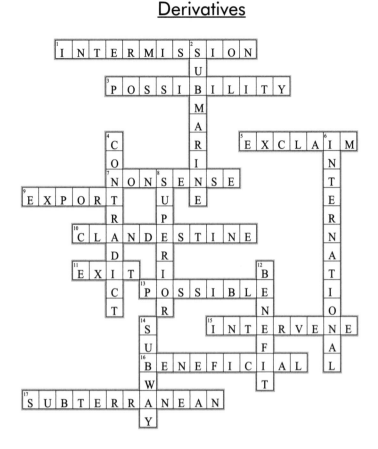

Grammar

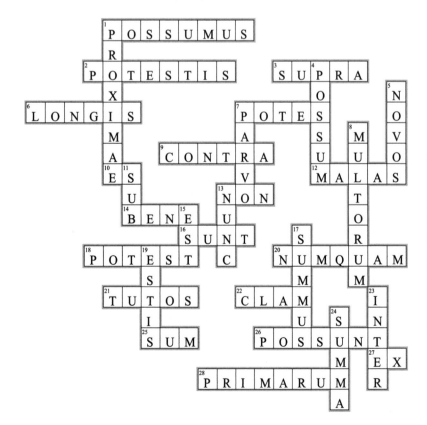

Hangman Lessons 11-15

NUNC AUT NUMQUAM
EXCELSIOR
ANTE BELLUM
SANCTUS SANCTUS SANCTUS
  DOMINUS DEUS SABAOTH
NOVUS ORDO SECLORUM

Lesson 16

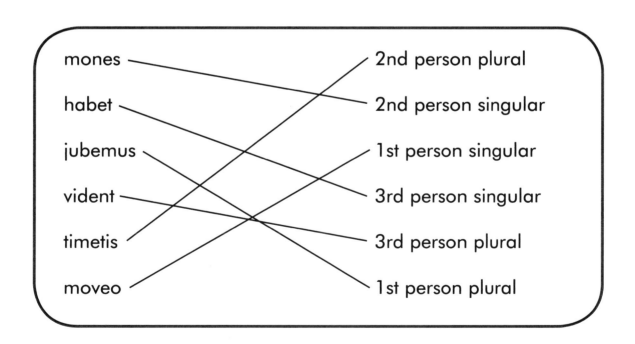

Derivatives

Grammar

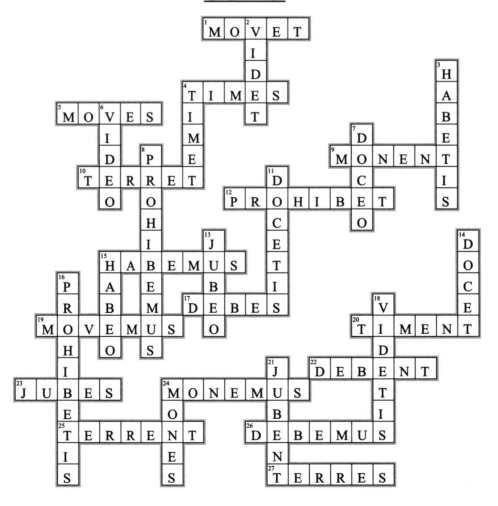

Lesson 17

PARSE STRINGS

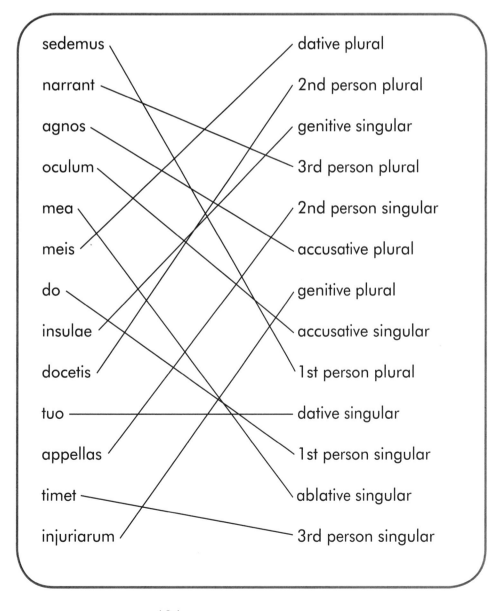

sedemus — 1st person plural

narrant — 3rd person plural

agnos — accusative plural

oculum — accusative singular

mea — ablative singular

meis — dative plural

do — 1st person singular

insulae — genitive singular

docetis — 2nd person plural

tuo — dative singular

appellas — 2nd person singular

timet — 3rd person singular

injuriarum — genitive plural

Derivatives

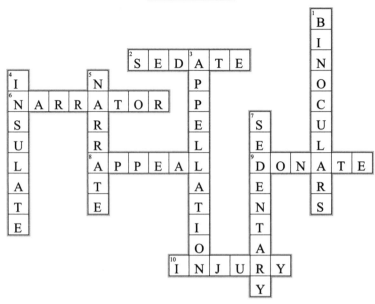

Grammar

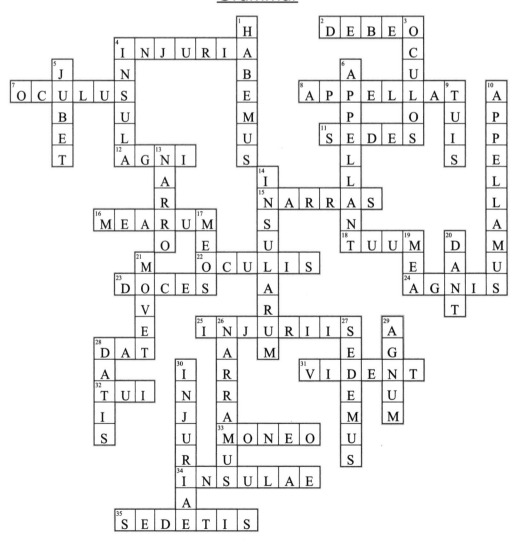

Lessons 18 -19

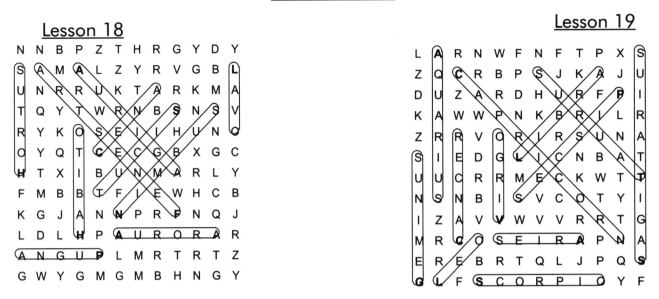

Lesson 18

Lesson 19

PARSE STRINGS

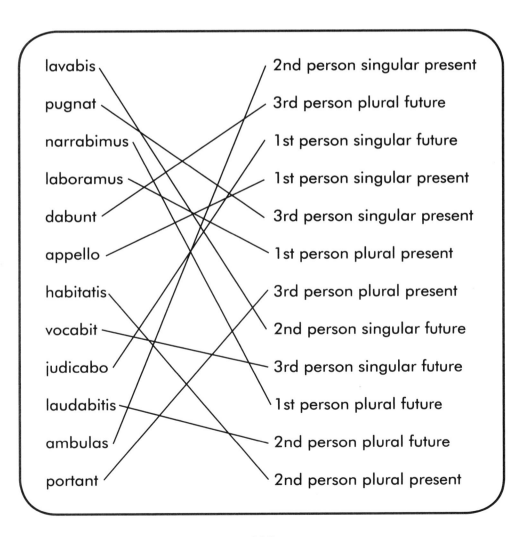

lavabis	2nd person singular present
pugnat	3rd person plural future
narrabimus	1st person singular future
laboramus	1st person singular present
dabunt	3rd person singular present
appello	1st person plural present
habitatis	3rd person plural present
vocabit	2nd person singular future
judicabo	3rd person singular future
laudabitis	1st person plural future
ambulas	2nd person plural future
portant	2nd person plural present

Derivatives

Lesson 20

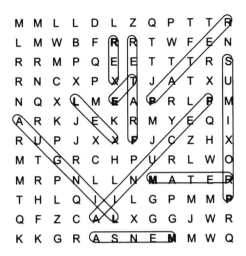

PARSE STRINGS

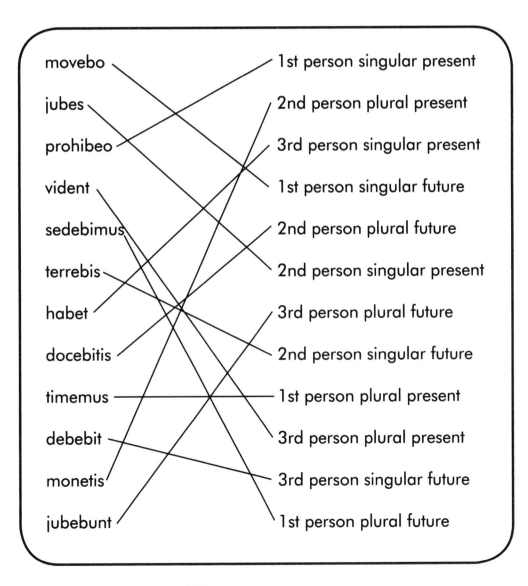

movebo   1st person singular present

jubes   2nd person plural present

prohibeo   3rd person singular present

vident   1st person singular future

sedebimus   2nd person plural future

terrebis   2nd person singular present

habet   3rd person plural future

docebitis   2nd person singular future

timemus   1st person plural present

debebit   3rd person plural present

monetis   3rd person singular future

jubebunt   1st person plural future

Derivatives

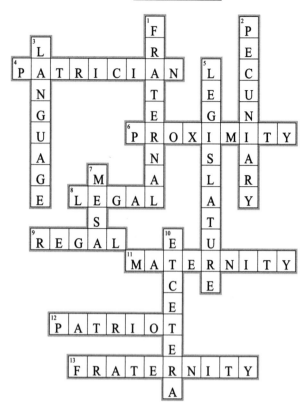

Hangman Lessons 16-20

RIDENT STOLIDI VERBA LATINA
ALMA MATER
AGNUS DEI QUI TOLLIS
    PECCATA MUNDI
VENI VIDI VICI
QUO VADIS

Grammar

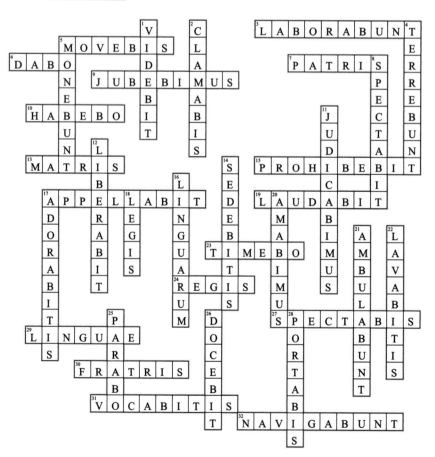

Lessons 21 - 22

Lesson 21

Lesson 22

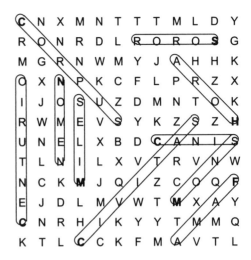

PARSE STRINGS

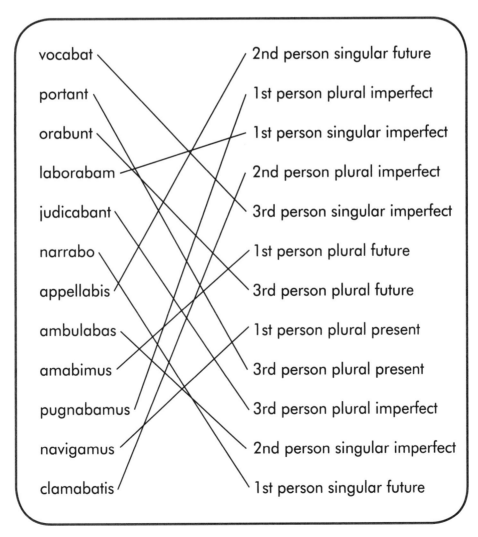

vocabat	2nd person singular future
portant	1st person plural imperfect
orabunt	1st person singular imperfect
laborabam	2nd person plural imperfect
judicabant	3rd person singular imperfect
narrabo	1st person plural future
appellabis	3rd person plural future
ambulabas	1st person plural present
amabimus	3rd person plural present
pugnabamus	3rd person plural imperfect
navigamus	2nd person singular imperfect
clamabatis	1st person singular future

Derivatives

(or CAPITOL)

(or CANARY)

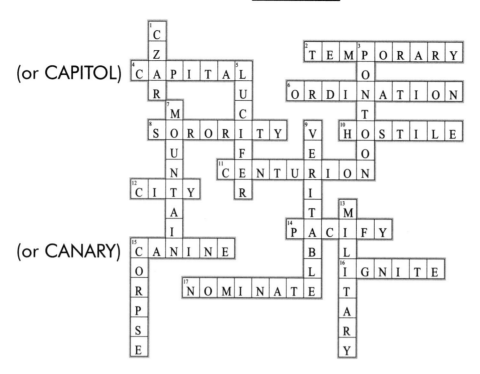

Grammar

Lesson 23

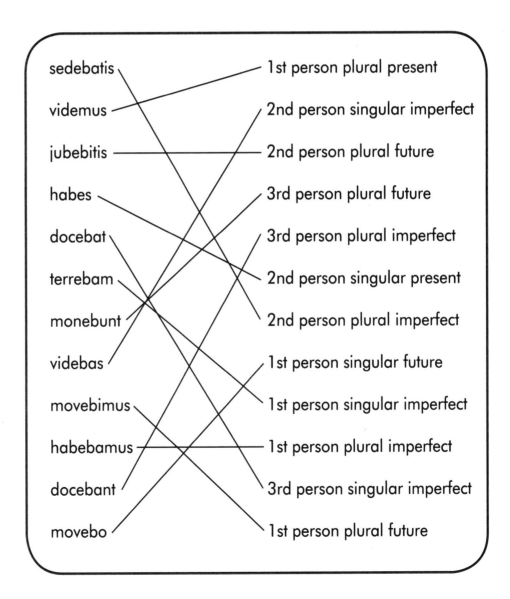

Derivatives

Grammar

Lessons 24 - 25

Lesson 24

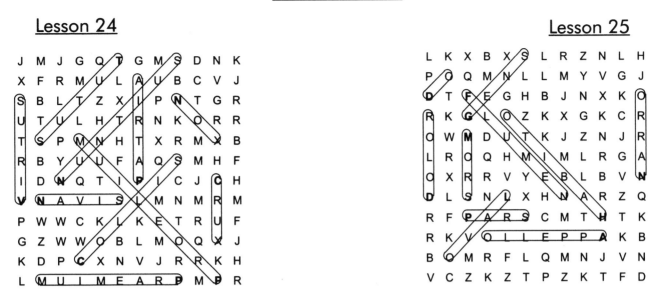

Lesson 25

PARSE STRINGS

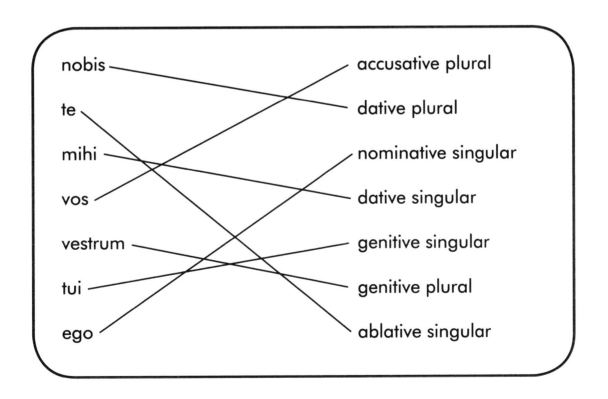

Derivatives

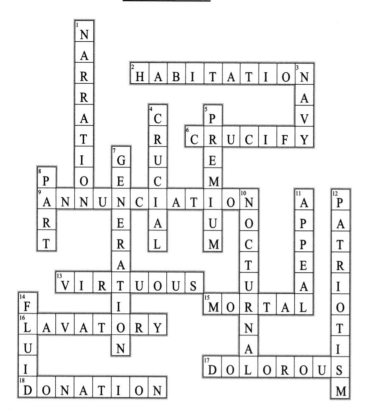

Grammar

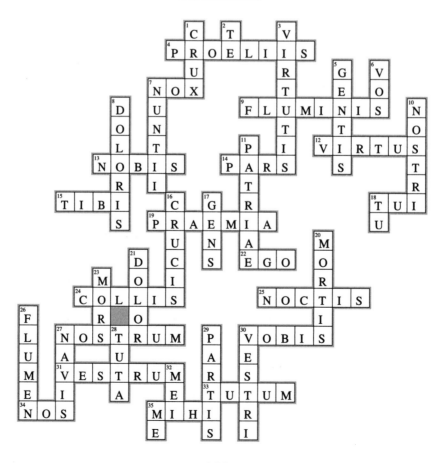

VOCABULARY and DERIVATIVES

VOCABULARY

Latin	English	Derivatives
adoro	I adore	*adoration*
aeternus -a -um	eternal, everlasting	*eternity*
agnus -i	lamb	
altus -a -um	high, deep	*altitude, altar*
ambulo	I walk	*ambulance*
amicus -i	friend	*amicable*
amo	I like, I love	*amorous, amateur*
animus -i	mind, spirit	*animated, animal*
annus -i	year	*annual, annals, anniversary*
ante	before	*antique*
appello	I speak to, I address	*appeal, appellation*
aqua -ae	water	*aquarium, aqueduct*
aquarius -i	The Water Carrier	
aquila -ae	eagle	*aquiline*
aries	The Ram	
auriga -ae	charioteer	
aurora -ae	dawn	*aurora borealis*
auxilium -i	help, aid	*auxiliary*
barbarus -i	barbarian	*barbaric*
bellum -i	war	*bellicose, belligerent, rebel*
bene	well	*benefit, benevolent*
bonus -a -um	good	*bonbon, bonny*
caelum -i	sky, heaven	*celestial*
Caesar -aris	Caesar	*tsar, czar*
campus -i	field, plain	*camp*
cancer	The Crab	
canis canis	dog	*canine*
capillus -i	hair	*capillary*
capricornus	The Goat	
caput -itis	head	*Capitol, capital, capitalize*
cena -ae	dinner	
centum	hundred	*cent, century, percent, centennial, centigrade*
centurio -onis	centurion	
certus -a -um	certain, sure	*certainly*
Christus -i	Christ	
cibus -i	food	*ciborium*
civitas -atis	state	*civil, civility, city, citizen, civilization*
clam	secretly	*clandestine*
clamo	I shout	*clamor, clamorous, exclamation, claim*
collis collis	hill	
contra	against	*contradict, contrary, contrast*
corona -ae	crown	*coronation*
corpus -oris	body	*corporal, corpse, corps, corporation*
crux crucis	cross	*crucifix, crucifixion, crucial*
culpa -ae	fault, crime	*culprit, culpable*
debeo	I owe, I ought	*debt, debtor, duty*
debitum -i	debt, trespass	*debit*
decem	ten	*December*
Deus -i	God	*deity*
discipulus -i	student	*disciple*
do	I give	*donate*
doceo	I teach	*docile, document, doctrine, indoctrinate*
dolor -oris	pain, sorrow	*dolorous, Via Dolorosa*
dominus -i	lord, master	*dominate, dominion*
donum -i	gift	*donate, donation, donor*
duo	two	*duet, dual, duo*
ecclesia -ae	church	*Ecclesiastes, ecclesiastical*
equus -i	horse	*equine, equestrian*
et	and	*etcetera*
ex	out of	*exit, extra*
fama -ae	fame, rumor	*famous, infamous*
femina -ae	woman	*feminine, female*
fenestra -ae	window	
filia -ae	daughter	*filial*
filius -i	son	*filial*
flumen -inis	river	*fluid, fluent*

fortuna -ae	fortune, chance	*fortune, fortunate*
forum -i	forum	
frater fratris	brother	*fraternal, fraternity*
frumentum -i	wheat, grain	
fuga -ae	flight	*fugitive, refugee, fugue*
Gallia -ae	Gaul	*Gallic*
gaudium -i	joy	*gaudy*
geminus (gemini)	The Twins	
gens gentis	tribe	*genitive, progeny, generate, gender*
gladius -i	short sword	*gladiator, gladiola*
gloria -ae	glory	*glorious, glorify*
gratia -ae	grace	*gracious, gratitude*
habeo	I have	*habit*
habito	I live in, I inhabit	*inhabit, habitation*
herba -ae	grass	*herb, herbal, herbivore*
Hispania -ae	Spain	*Hispanic*
homo -inis	man, person	*homicide, homo sapiens*
hora -ae	hour	*horoscope*
hortus -i	garden	*horticulture*
hostis hostis	enemy	*host, hostile, hostility*
ignis ignis	fire	*ignite, ignition, igneous*
imperator -oris	general, commander	*imperative*
imperium -i	command, empire	*imperial, emperor, empire, imperious*
injuria -ae	injury	*injurious*
insula -ae	island	*insulate, insular*
inter	between	*interior, intermission, intergalactic, interlude*
ira -ae	anger	*ire, irate*
Italia -ae	Italy	*italics*
Jesus	Jesus	
jubeo	I order, I command	
judico	I judge, I consider	*judiciary, justice*
laboro	I work	*laborious, laboratory*
laudo	I praise	*laud, laudable*
lavo	I wash	*lavatory, lava, lave*
legatus -i	lieutenant, envoy	*delegate*
legio -onis	legion	*legionary*
leo	The Lion	*leonine*
lex legis	law	*legal, legislature*
libero	I free	*liberate, liberal, liberty*
libra	The Scales	
lingua -ae	tongue, language	*language, bilingual, linguistic*
locus -i	place	*local, location*
longus -a -um	long	*longitude*
ludus -i	game, sport, school	*ludicrous*
luna -ae	moon	*lunar, lunacy, lunatic*
lux lucis	light	*lucid, Lucifer*
magnus -a -um	large, great	*magnify, magnificent*
malus -a -um	bad	*malady, maladjusted, malice, dismal*
Maria -ae	Mary	*Mary*
mater matris	mother	*maternal, matrimony*
memoria -ae	memory	*memorial, memorize*
mensa -ae	table	*mesa*
meus -a -um	my	
miles -itis	soldier	*military, militia*
mille	thousand	*mile, million, milligram, millennium*
moneo	I warn, I advise	*monitor, admonish*
mons montis	mountain	*mount*
mora -ae	delay	*moratorium*
mors mortis	death	*mortal, mortality, immortal*
moveo	I move	*movie, remove, move, movable*
multus -a -um	much, many	*multiply, multitude*
mundus -i	world, mankind	*mundane*
murus -i	wall	*mural*
narro	I tell	*narrator*
nauta -ae	sailor	*nautilus, nautical*
navigo	I sail, navigate	*navigate, navigation*
navis navis	ship	*navy, naval*
nimbus -i	cloud	
nomen -inis	name	*nominate, noun, nominative*
non	not	*nonsense*
novem	nine	*November*
novus -a -um	new	*novel, novice, innovate, renovate*

nox noctis	night	*nocturnal, equinox*
numquam	never	
nunc	now	
nuntius -i	messenger, message	*announce, pronounce*
occupo	I seize	*occupy, occupation*
octo	eight	*October*
oculus -i	eye	*ocular, binocular*
oppidum -i	town	
ordo ordinis	rank	*order, ordain*
oro	I pray, I give a speech	*oratory, orator*
paro	I prepare	*preparation*
pars partis	part	*particle, particular, partial*
parvus -a -um	small, insignificant	
pater patris	father	*paternal, patrician*
patria -ae	country, fatherland	*patriot, patriotic*
pax pacis	peace	*pacify, pacific, pacifier*
peccatum -i	mistake, sin	*impeccable, peccadillo*
pecunia -ae	money, wealth	*pecuniary, peculiar (from **pecus,** cow)*
pisces	The Fish	
plenus -a -um	full	*plenary, plenty, plentiful*
pons pontis	bridge	*pontoon*
populus -i	people	*population, popular*
porto	I carry	*portable, transport, export, import*
post	after	*posterior, posterity*
praemium -i	reward	*premium*
primus -a -um	first	*primary, prime*
proelium -i	battle	
prohibeo	I prevent	*prohibit*
proximus -a -um	nearest, next	*proximity, approximate*
summus -a -um	highest, greatest	*summit, sum*
puella -ae	girl	
pugna -ae	fight	*pugnacious, repugnant*
pugno	I fight	*pugnacious*
quattuor	four	*quart, quarter, quartet (from **quartus**, fourth)*
quinque	five	*quintuplets (from **quintus**, fifth)*
regina -ae	queen	
regnum -i	kingdom	
rex regis	king	*regal, Tyrannosaurus Rex*
Roma -ae	Rome	*Roman*
saepe	often	
sagittarius	The Archer	
sanctus -a -um	holy, saintly	*sanctify, sanctification, sanctuary*
scorpio	The Scorpion	
secundus -a -um	second	*secondary, second*
sedeo	I sit	*sedentary, sediment, sedate*
semper	always	
septem	seven	*September*
servus -i	slave	*service, servant, servile*
sex	six	*sextet*
sicut	as	
signum -i	sign, standard	*signal, signature, insignia, design*
silva -ae	forest	*sylvan, Pennsylvania, Transylvania*
socius -i	ally, comrade	*social, society*
solus -a -um	alone, only	*solitary, solitude, solo*
soror -oris	sister	*sorority*
specto	I look at	*spectacle, inspect, spectator, spectacular*
stella -ae	star	*stellar*
sub	under	*submarine, subway*
supero	I overcome, I conquer	*superior*
supra	above	*supranational*
taurus	The Bull	
telum -i	weapon	
tempus -oris	time	*temporal, tempo, tense*
tergum -i	back	
terra -ae	land, earth	*terrestrial, terrain, territory, Mediterranean*
terreo	I frighten	*terrify*
tertius -a -um	third	*tertiary*
timeo	I fear	*timid, intimidate*
toga -ae	toga	*toga*
totus -a -um	whole	*total*
tres	three	*trio, triangle*
tutus -a -um	safe	

tuus -a -um	your (singular)	
unda -ae	wave	*undulate, inundate*
unus	one	*unity, universe, union, unit, unique*
urbs urbis	city, Rome	*urban, suburb*
ursa -ae	(she-) bear	*Ursa Major, Ursa Minor*
vallum -i	wall, rampart	
ventus -i	wind	*vent, ventilate*
verbum -i	word	*verbal, verbose, verb*
veritas -atis	truth	*verity, verify, very*
via -ae	road, way	*viaduct, via*
victoria -ae	victory	*victorious*
video	I see	*evident, vision, video*
vinum -i	wine	*vine, vineyard*
virgo	The Virgin	
virtus -utis	virtue, courage	*virtuous, virtue*
vita -ae	life	*vital, vitamin*
voco	I call	*vocal, vocation*
vox vocis	voice	*vocal, vocation*

DEFINITIONS of DERIVATIVES

admonish: to gently reprove, caution, or warn
adoration: great love or devotion
adore: to show great love or devotion
adverb: a part of speech that modifies a verb or adjective
altar: a platform for worship or sacrifice
altimeter: a device for measuring altitude
altitude: height
amateur: one who does something for pleasure, not profit
ambulance: a vehicle for carrying the sick or wounded
ambulatory: able to walk
amiable: good-natured
amicable: friendly
amorous: full of love
animal: a living being that is not plant or fungus
animated: lively; in the form of a cartoon
animation: the process or result of animating
annals: a yearly history
anniversary: the yearly commemoration of an event
announce: to proclaim the existence or arrival of
annual: yearly
annunciation: the process or result of announcing
antebellum: the period before the American Civil War
anticipate: to realize beforehand; to look forward to
antique: of an earlier period; furniture or furnishings over 100 years old
appeal: an urgent request or supplication; to make an urgent request or supplication
appellation: a name, title, or designation
approximate: almost exact or correct
aquarium: a tank for keeping sea creatures
aquatic: relating to water, being in water
aqueduct: a channel for transporting water by gravity
aquiline: having to do with eagles
aurora borealis: the northern lights
automobile: a horseless carriage
auxiliary: supplementary, supporting
barbarian: a people considered by another to be without civilization
barbaric: having to with or having the qualities of barbarians
bellicose: warlike
belligerent: threatening war
beneficial: of benefit
benefit: advantage; something that promotes well-being
benevolent: characterized by doing good
bilingual: speaking or expressed in two languages
binocular: having to do with both eyes
binoculars: an optical magnifier for two eyes
bonbon: a candy with a soft center
bonny: pretty, excellent
boon: jolly
camp: a place where temporary shelters are set up
campus: the grounds of a school, college, or university
canary: a yellow songbird
canine: having to do with dogs
capillary: as fine as a hair
capital: wealth accumulated in a business; seat of government
capitalize: to fund a business; to take advantage

Capitol: the temple of Jupiter at Rome; the U.S. Congress building complex
celestial: heavenly
cent: a hundredth part of a dollar
centennial: a celebration of the 100th year of something
centigrade: a system of measuring temperature having 100 degrees between the boiling and freezing point of water
centimeter: a hundredth part of a meter
centipede: a worm-like insect with many legs
centurion: a Roman soldier and member of a century (corps of 100 men)
century: one hundred years
certain: sure
certainly: with certainty
Christian: having to do with the Christian religion; member of the Christian religion
Christmas: the celebration of the birth of Christ
ciborium: the canopy over an altar; a receptacle for eucharist wafers
citizen: a member of a state
city: a sizeable center of population
civil: having to do with the citizenry
civility: politeness
civilization: the type of culture of a state in a given period; a relatively advanced state of cultural development
claim: to demand or take for one's own
clamor: a loud outcry
clamorous: having or full of clamor
clandestine: secret
constellation: a group of stars that forms a picture
contemporary: of the same time period as
contradict: to express opposition; to deny
contradiction: a denial; an inconsistency
contrary: opposite or different
contrast: to compare unlike things
coronation: the crowning of a king or queen
corps: a body of men in an armed force
corporal: having to do with the body; an army officer
corporation: a business chartered as an independent legal entity
corpse: a dead body
crucial: extremely significant, vital
crucifix: the amulet of the cross
crucifixion: a method of execution by fixing to a cross
culpable: guilty
culprit: the guilty party
czar (tsar): the monarch of pre-revolutionary Russia
debit: an item of debt in an account
debt: money or favors owed
debtor: one who owes a debt
December: the tenth month of the Roman calendar
decimal: based on the number ten
decimate: to destroy
deify: to make a god
deity: a god
delegate: to assign authority; a representative at a conference
design: to conceive or fashion
disciple: a student or follower
discipline: training; controlled behavior
disclaim: to deny or renounce claim
dismal: dreary; lacking merit
divine: having to do with a god or gods
docile: teachable; yielding to supervision or control
doctor: one trained and licensed in medical practice; one holding an advanced academic degree

doctrine: an official teaching

document: written information

dolorous: exhibiting grief, sorrow, or pain

domain: a realm

dominate: to exercise authority over

domination: the process or result of dominating

dominion: sovereignty

donate: to give to a fund or cause

donation: the process or result of donating

donor: one who donates

dual: double

duet: a pair of performers; a piece of music for two performers

duo: two people doing something in close association

duty: an obligation or service

Ecclesiastes: a book of the Bible

ecclesiastical: having to do with church or churches

emperor: the monarch of an empire

empire: an extended state consisting of a nation and its conquered territories

equestrian: having to do with riding horses

equine: having to do with horses

equinox: the two times of the year when day and night are of more or less equal length

etcetera: and so on

eternal: existing forever

eternity: an endless or seemingly endless period of time

evidence: a thing helpful in forming a conclusion; a thing indicative of something

evident: apparent

exclaim: to shout out, as in surprise

exclamation: the process or result of exclaiming

exit: a way out

export: to send out of a country

extra: additional

extraterrestrial: from beyond the Earth

fame: great renown

famous: having or full of fame

female: of or having to do with the female sex

feminine: having the qualities of a female

filial: having to do with duties of a son or daughter toward a parent

fluent: free in expression

fluid: having the qualities of a liquid

fortunate: lucky

fortune: luck; great wealth

forum: an assembly, real or virtual, for the exchange of ideas

fraternal: having to do with brothers

fraternity: an association of men or male students

fruit: a type of produce; the result or product of some activity

fugitive: one fleeing prosecution or detention

gaudy: cheaply showy

Gaul: the ancient nation of the Gauls, in large part coincident with modern France

gender: the grammatical categories masculine, feminine, and neuter

generate: to yield or produce

generation: the process or result of generating

genitive: the grammatical case indicating possession or attribute

gladiator: a combatant of the Roman arena who fights with a short sword

gladiola: a sword-shaped flower

glorify: to exalt, worship, or honor

glorious: wonderful

grace: favor; effortless beauty of form or movement

gracious: kind, tactful
grateful: feeling or exhibiting gratitude
gratitude: a feeling of thankfulness
habit: a compulsive action
habitation: a place of abode; the act of inhabiting
herb: leaves of a plant used as medicine or in cooking
herbal: of or having to do with herbs
herbicide: a plant killer
herbivore: a plant eater
Hispanic: having to do with Spanish culture in the Americas
homicide: the killing of a human
homo sapiens: the human species
horticulture: the science or practice of plant culture
host: a horde
hostile: of or having the characteristics of an enemy
hostility: hostile feelings or acts
hour: the twenty-fourth part of the day
igneous: of or relating to fire
ignite: to set on fire
ignition: the process or result of igniting
immortal: undying or unable to die
impeccable: perfect, unblemished
imperative: urgent or extremely necessary
imperial: having to do with empire
imperious: arrogantly domineering
import: to bring into a country
infamous: of great negative repute
infamy: the condition of being infamous
inhabit: to reside in
injurious: harmful
injury: harm, damage
inspect: to look at closely
insular: isolated; having to do with or having the characteristics of an island
insulate: to shield or protect from outside influences
intergalactic: among the galaxies
interior: of the inside
interlude: a period of time between two events
intermission: a period of time between segments of a performance
international: having to do with many nations
interregnum: the period of time that a throne is unoccupied between two reigns
intervene: to come between two things
intimidate: to cause fear in another
inundate: to flood
irate: extremely angry
Italian: having to do with Italy
judge: to make a critical decision; one who judges
judicial: having to do with judges, courts, and laws
judiciary: having to do with the courts
justice: fairness
labor: work; physical or mental exertion
laboratory: a place for scientific work or research
laborious: involving strenuous labor
language: spoken communication; the speech of a particular people
laud: to praise
laudable: worthy of praise
lava: a flow of molten magma from a volcano
lavatory: the bathroom

lave: to wash

legal: conforming to the law

legality: the state or quality of being legal

legate: an official emissary

legation: a diplomatic mission below an embassy

legion: a corps of the Roman army consisting of 4000-5000 men

legionary: a member of a legion

legislature: a law-making body

liberal: not limited by orthodoxy; generous

liberate: to free

liberty: freedom

linguistic: having to do with language

local: of a particular region

locality: neighborhood

location: the place where something is

longitude: imaginary lines that run north and south from pole to pole on a globe

lucid: clear

Lucifer: Satan

ludicrous: ridiculous

lunacy: insanity, madness

lunar: having to do with the moon

lunatic: a madman

magnanimous: generous, big-hearted

magnificent: extremely impressive or beautiful

magnify: to make or make appear larger

magnitude: size

magnum: an oversized bottle of wine; an overcharged bullet

maladjusted: poorly adapted to an activity or society

malady: disease

malice: ill will

malicious: intending harm

maternal: having to do with mothers or motherhood

maternity: motherhood

matrimony: marriage

Mediterranean: the sea between Europe and Africa

memorial: something honoring the memory of something or someone

memorize: to commit to memory

mesa: a flat-topped landform typical of the American southwest

mile: a distance of 5280 feet

militarize: to make material

military: having to do with the armed forces

millennium: a period of a thousand years

milligram: a thousandth of a gram

million: a thousand thousands

monitor: to observe and gather information on an activity

moratorium: the temporary cessation of an activity

mortal: having to do with that which will die

mortality: the quality or condition of being mortal

motor: an engine that imparts motion

mount: to get or put on top of

mountain: the greatest and steepest of the uplifted landforms

movable: able to be moved

move: to be in motion; to change the location of

movie: a moving picture; a film

multiplication: the process or result of multiplying

multiply: to increase the number, amount, or degree of

multitude: a great number

mundane: ordinary, commonplace
mural: a painting on a wall
narrate: to tell a story or event
narration: the process or result of narrating
narrative: a story, narrated account
narrator: a person who tells a story or event
nautical: having to do with seafaring
nautilus: an ancient chambered mollusk
naval: having to do with ships or a navy
navigate: to steer a ship or plane
navigation: the process or result of navigating
navy: a nation's ships; a dark blue color
nocturnal: of or having to do with the night
nominate: to put one's name up for something
nominative: the grammatical case expressing the subject of a verb
nonsense: meaningless ideas or statements
noun: the part of speech that names things
novel: new and unusual
novelty: something that is new and unusual
November: the ninth month of the Roman calendar
novice: a beginner
occupation: a job or professional activity; the process or result of occupying
occupy: to seize control of; to inhabit a dwelling
octet: an eight-member group; a piece of music for eight performers
October: the eighth month of the Roman calendar
octopus: an eight-tentacled sea creature
ocular: having to do with the eye
oration: public speech
orator: a public speaker
oratorical: having to do with or having the qualities of oratory
oratory: the art of public speaking
ordain: to confer holy orders on
order: a condition of logical or meaningful arrangement
ordination: the act of ordaining or the state of being ordained
pacific: peaceful
pacifier: a device for pacifying
pacify: to make peaceful
part: a segment of a whole
partial: incomplete, being a part of
particle: a very small object
particular: of a specific person, group, or category
paternal: having to do with fathers
patriarch: the male head of a family
patrician: a member of the Roman noble class
patriot: one who loves his or her country
patriotic: showing a love for one's country
patriotism: the love of country
peccadillo: a small sin
peculiar: odd; distinct
pecuniary: having to do with money
Pennsylvania: a state in the northeastern United States ("Penn's wood")
percent: expressed in hundredths
plenary: complete; fully attended
plentiful: abundant
plenty: abundance
pontoon: a floating structure
popular: of or having to do with the people; appealing to many people

153

population: the people of a city, state, or country
populous: full of people
portable: able to be carried
possibility: something that is possible
possible: able to exist or happen
posterior: located behind or to the rear
posterity: the generations that come after; future generations
postscript: a statement added to the end of a letter or document
prelude: an introductory performance, movement or event
premium: of the highest quality; a prize; an additional payment
preparation: getting ready, making in advance
preparatory: functioning as a preparation
prepare: to make ready
primal: first in time; of first importance
primary: principal; first in rank
prime: first in quality or value
primordial: first in order or sequence
progeny: offspring
prohibit: to forbid by authority
prohibition: the process or result of prohibiting
pronounce: to speak, utter; to declare officially
proximity: nearness
puerile: childish
pugnacious: in a fighting spirit
quart: the fourth part of a gallon
quarter: a fourth part of something
quartet: a group of four
quintet: a group of five performers; a piece of music for five performers
quintuplets: five babies born at the same time of the same mother
rebel: to resist or defy authority; one who rebels
rebellion: an act of rebelling
refugee: one who seeks refuge
regal: like a king or queen; befitting royalty
regalia: the trappings of royalty
reign: to rule; a period of rule
remove: to take away
repugnant: disgusting
revitalize: to reinvigorate
Roman: of or having to do with Rome
sanctification: the process or result of sanctifying
sanctify: to make holy
sanctity: the state or condition of being holy
sanctuary: a place of refuge; a chapel
second: next in order after the first; a 60th of a minute
secondary: of second rank or importance
sedate: calm
sedentary: involving much sitting
sediment: solids that settle out of a flowing liquid
sedimentary: of or having to do with sediment
September: the seventh month of the Roman calendar
servant: one employed to perform services
service: work done for others
servile: slave-like
servitude: slavery
sextet: a six-member performing group; a piece of music for six performers
sign: something indicative of something; an identifying placard or notice
signal: an indicator

signature: one's name written by oneself; a characteristic mark
social: having to do with society
society: a group of humans united by shared interests and institutions
solitary: alone
solitude: the condition of being alone
solo: a performance or activity by a single person; a piece of music for a single performer
sorority: an association of women or female students
spectacle: a remarkable sight
spectacular: remarkable, unusual
spectator: one who watches an event or performance
stellar: having to do with a star; outstanding
submarine: an underwater boat; having to do with undersea travel or activity
subterranean: underground
suburb: outlying part of a city
suburban: having to do with suburbs
subway: an underground railway
sum: the whole amount, quantity, or number
summit: the peak or highest point
superior: excellent
supernatural: outside the natural world
supranational: beyond the authority of a nation
supreme: highest
sylvan: having to do with the forest
tempest: a violent storm
tempo: pace
temporal: having to do with time
temporary: existing for a limited period of time
tense: the grammatical category having to do with the time frame of verbs
terrain: land as defined by its features
terrestrial: of or having to do with the Earth
terrific: very good
terrify: to instill terror
territory: an area of land defined by its boundaries
tertiary: third in order or importance
timid: easily frightened
timidity: the condition of being timid
toga: the formal garment of the Roman patrician
total: complete, whole
totality: the complete amount or quantity of
transport: to convey from one place to another
Transylvania: a region of central Europe beyond the German forests
triangle: a three-sided polygon
trio: a group of three; a piece of music for three performers
undulate: to move in a wave-like motion
union: the state or condition of being united
unique: one-of-a-kind
unit: the elementary part of a whole
unity: the state or condition of being one
universe: the totality of matter and energy
urban: of or having to do with the city
Ursa Major: a constellation ("the Great Bear")
Ursa Minor: a constellation ("the Little Bear")
vent: to allow to escape, especially gasses
ventilate: to allow air to flow through
verb: the part of speech expressing action or state of being
verbal: having to do with verbs; spoken
verbose: excessively wordy

verdict: the judgment in a trial
verify: to confirm as true
verily: truly
veritable: genuine
very: to a great degree
via: by way of
viaduct: a bridge on piers or towers
victorious: having victory
video: relating to television
vine: a weak-stemmed plant that derives support from climbing or creeping
vineyard: a farm for wine grapes
virtue: excellence of character
virtuous: having or full of virtue
vision: sight
visual: having to do with sight; seen
vital: extremely important
vitality: vigor and energy
vitamin: a natural substance essential to health
vocabulary: a list of words
vocal: having to do with speaking or singing
vocation: an occupation as a calling
voice: the sound produced by the vocal organs; the grammatical category of verbs expressing the role of the subject
wall: the vertical elements of a building; a defensive structure